Revised and Updated
Second Edition

The 4-Lane Expressway to STRESS MANAGEMENT

How to conquer stress bodily, emotionally, intellectually and spiritually

Ajay Shukla

UNICORN BOOKS Pvt. Ltd.

Publisher
UNICORN BOOKS
F-2/16, Ansari Road, Daryaganj, New Delhi-110002
☎ 011-23275434, 23262683, 23250704 • *Fax:* 011-23257790
E-mail: info@unicornbooks.in • *Website:* www.unicornbooks.in

Branch : Mumbai
23-25, Zaoba Wadi Thakurdwar, Mumbai-401002
☎ 022-22010941, 022-22053387
E-mail: rapidex@bom5.vsnl.net.in

Showroom :
★ **PM Publications,** New Delhi
- 10-B, Netaji Subhash Marg, Daryaganj
  New Delhi-110002
- 6686, Khari Baoli, Delhi-110006

ISBN 978-81-7806-200-6
The 4-Lane Expressway to Stress Management (English)

Edition: 2013

Printed at : *Param Offsetters, Okhla, New Delhi-110020*

Preface

For a long time, I had been introspecting about what makes me tense and unhappy. In the last few years, after deep thought, reading voraciously on the subject, and observing my own behaviour as well as that of others, I began receiving certain answers. The basic reason was that I, and others like me, had not realised that we were under stress and how it was affecting us. Being ignorant about how stress works, I had made no conscious and sustained effort to be free of stress and had not actively strived for happiness.

Perhaps, we are not even aware that happiness requires our own efforts. We expect happiness to come to us from some external and indeterminate source. But that does not happen. Now, especially after reading the *Bhagavad Gita,* I have realised that nothing is going to come to us from outside. We have to make our own efforts.

The *Bhagavad Gita* (Chapter VI, Shloka 6) says that man is his own best friend and his own worst enemy. As such, you should not do anything that may put you in a state of peril.

There is a saying that God helps those who help themselves. The fundamental meaning is the same: Even God cannot help those who become their own enemy. So if you treat yourself well, as a good friend, physically as well as psychologically, happiness is yours. Nobody else from outside can bring you happiness. Only YOU can do this. And you can, if you want to, and aim for it. It all depends on how *you* are treating yourself.

I have written this book from personal experience, with a firm belief that if you *really* want to, you can remain free from stress and be healthy and happy. Having organised workshops, and given lectures on the subject for the past few years, I am even more convinced that happiness can be achieved by adopting a certain way of life, by developing a certain way of thinking and feeling. It needs changes in outlook and attitudes. By thus moulding yourself, you can almost change your own fate. This *can* be done. YOU can do it. It all depends on YOU.

I cannot control your stress. Neither can this book, nor any other book or person, bring you happiness. Only YOU can. In fact you CAN. I can only show you the way, give you a few tips, but you have to take the initiative, and you have to make the effort to walk this road that leads to happiness.

In fact, you have a right to be happy.

I have no doubt that this book will help you get rid of the negative effects of stress and live a healthier and happier life.

–Ajay Shukla

Contents

Introduction

Stress can be defined as a form of tension or strain in the body or the mind for which there is no release or outlet. When under stress, one is like a car in the neutral gear with the accelerator on, trying to exert internally, but unable to do so.

Stress is not something that affects us from outside. It is not something acquired only by some unfortunate individuals. It is an integral part of the physical and mental system in each of us. We all have inherited it during the course of evolution. It is an essential, rather a vital, ingredient for the normal functioning of the body and, hence, inescapable. It helps us in our survival on a sustained basis.

Nevertheless, when left unchecked and uncontrolled, it eats into our psyche and erodes our immune system, almost like AIDS. It acts as a silent killer and is a catalyst for several diseases.

Over a period of time, the negative effects of stress make us weak and vulnerable, and leave us an easy prey for all sorts of physical and psychological problems. It has been conclusively proved that stress is one of the biggest threats to our physical and mental health.

As civilisations progress, complications and concomitant tensions inevitably increase, and will increase in future also. Stress cannot be avoided but, yes, it can be managed in a way that it does not become a source of trouble.

In order to understand how the stress factor came into being and became a part of our psychosomatic system, it is necessary to briefly understand the process of evolution of man. In this book, I will first discuss how the stress factor came into human life.

Once we have understood how stress has come into being as an integral part of our system, we will examine its perceptible symptoms. Then we will see how it affects our health. Thereafter, we will discuss the *4-Lane Path* to manage our stress.

In the final chapter, we will discuss how to remain happy.

The Origins of Man

We all are conscious of how our body looks like. We may also know how it functions. Many of us are also quite conscious of our own intellectual capabilities, and of our attitudes. But why our body, and our mind, functions in the way it does, we are often not aware. We know quite well about the society in which we live. But we often wonder why the other person, or the society as a corporate body, acts in a particular way. We must realize that what we are today is the culmination of a very long process of evolution. The way living beings are today, the way we think and act is out of conditioning through the process of evolution that has taken place about 5 billion years ago. Our roots lie in our past. In order to understand why we are the way we are, it is essential to know of our origin from the time of the creation of the universe. We must know how life came into being and how we human beings evolved into our present shape. Only then we will be able to comprehend the various facets of our personality, and the way our body and our mind function.

There are fundamentally two versions about the creation of the universe and the origin of life – the mythological version and scientific theories. Naturally, these two versions are totally different. Mythological and religious versions all over the world basically portray the creation of the universe as an act of God. These hold that God created this world and also created various life forms as a conscious act.

The Big Bang

Scientific theories are diametrically opposite. The modern scientific theory of creation is known as the Big Bang theory. It says that just before the creation of the universe, the entire matter of the universe was concentrated at one place, forming what is known as a Black Hole. A Black Hole is a concentration of matter with tremendous amount of heat energy. Due to the excessive mass, its gravitational power is so great that it attracts anything and everything that comes near it and 'consumes' it. This further increases its mass and hence its gravitational pull. Ultimately, its gravitational pull becomes so immense that even light cannot escape it; hence it is called a Black Hole.

The Big Bang theory describes the phenomenon of creation of the universe as due to the explosion of a Black Hole, and hence is called the Big Bang theory. The explosion of the Black Hole occurred because a time came when the mass of the Black Hole became so excessive that its gravitational force could no longer hold the entire matter together, and because of very excessive heat energy, it exploded. This explosion of the Black Hole led to matter and energy spewing out all over space (energy getting transformed into matter as per Einstein's theorem) leading to the formation of galaxies of heavenly bodies. Thus were formed suns (stars) and planets. The Big Bang occurred around 10-12 billion years ago.

Divine Manifestation

Though mythologies all over the world differ from scientific theories, it is strange to find a rather similar line of thought expressed in the *Rig Veda*. The tenth *mandala* of the *Rig Veda* describes the phenomenon of creation in a poetic way as the awakening or manifestation of Brahman out of its dormancy (sleep). It says that out of its own volition and power, Brahman transformed from its non-being state to the being state, causing creation of this existence out of itself. Before this event it was absolutely dark everywhere and nothing existed anywhere. All that existed was heat energy or *tapas.* The formation of the universe was out of the unveiling of this energy.

To quote from the *Rig Veda* (Mandala X, Sukti 129):

In the state of flood/flux (beginning) there was neither matter nor non-matter, neither being nor non-being. At that time there was neither the world nor space (neither the sky nor anything beyond). There was no life anywhere or any source of pleasure. What was there? And where? What was the power? At that time even the solemn water did not exist.

At that time there was neither death nor immortality. There was neither the night nor the notion of day. At that time only one, Brahman, *imbued with life energy in its nature, breathed, and nothing else existed.*

It was all darkness everywhere (darkness hidden in darkness) and existence was unknown (formless and fluid). With tapas *self-exertion (power of heat), out of nothingness (void) emerged* Brahman, *without external cause or action.*

This caused the conception of the creation of the universe. It formed the seed of the entire creation. Sages thought over this and found the cause of matter out of non-matter.

Who knows the entire truth and who can speak about this creation? What were the causative factors of this creation? The gods have originated after the creation. Who knows the one from which this world was created?

It is not known how this existence has come up. He only knows the one who created this or unveiled it. Does He bear it or not?

This description of creation comes very close to the scientific theory of the creation of the universe, that is, the Big Bang theory.

The Origins of Life

Earth was also one of these celestial bodies. At the time of creation it was like a ball of fire. It took a few million years for earth to cool and take a solid shape. Space was full of small bodies that kept colliding with earth, like comets and meteors. These brought different chemicals and due to extreme heat on earth led to a chain of chemical reactions. The reaction that led to the formation of water on earth was one of the most vital events of that time.

There is also a theory that says that water was not formed on earth. This theory says that there was a comet containing water, which collided with earth, bringing water on earth. Water, with the property to dissolve most chemicals, facilitated chemical reactions that led to formation of different and complex compounds. For the first four billion years after its formation, there was no life on earth.

Formation of amino-nucleic acids is supposed to have been the precursor of life on earth. This formation perhaps occurred around Black Smokers, volcanic chimney-like structures found at the ocean floor. They emit black scalding water, gushing out from the core of the earth. Microbes such as bacteria have been found at such places. Many scientists believe that these are the places where life on earth could have begun.

Somewhere in such a spot, without any known provocation, a group of amino-nucleic acids must have suddenly moved forward on their own. They repeated the process and survived in the attempt. Initially they fluctuated between the living and the non-living forms. Then, something made them capable of continuing existence in the living form. And so, life came into being out of a dynamic chemical process. The greatest event of all times, the origin of life, had occurred, without causing even a whimper anywhere.

This was about six billion years ago, that is, about four billion years after earth came into existence.

Somehow, these living beings were imbued with a power or spirit called the survival instinct. Life is nothing else, but the sustenance and supremacy of the survival instinct. It was this survival instinct that compelled these living beings to adjust according to their environment. The survival instinct also made them perpetuate their existence in the living form. Once they had come into being as a life form, these clusters of chemicals started adjusting themselves to their environment for survival. There was an internal force exerted within these living beings, provoked by the survival instinct, which forced them to change and adapt according to their environment. This internal force was stress.

The survival instinct activated stress within these living beings in their endeavour to adapt themselves to their environment in order to ensure survival.

> *The first time that stress was ever exerted inside a living being was when life itself originated.*

That was also the beginning of the process of evolution. These living beings needed to survive their environment and were required to be fitter to survive. Hence, the primeval life forms evolved continuously, improving and adapting themselves in the process of evolution with a single objective, to be in a better position to survive. Since then, the instinct to survive has continuously strengthened and carried the process of evolution ahead. Thus, once life came into existence, stress has been the force behind evolution, and an integral part of our body mechanism.

The instinct to survive is the basic character of all living beings. It has been the single most important factor in the process of evolution and the most important cause of the development of body and mind in all life forms. It is only because of this deeply ingrained instinct in every single living cell that we have all the various forms of plant and animal life on this planet today. The entire phenomenon of life that we see on earth today is nothing but a manifestation of the endeavour of that instinct to survive.

Evolution Through Stress

The quest for survival was the guiding principle in the process of evolution of the body and the mind. For almost one billion years or more, life on earth consisted only of microbes and single cellular beings. These were confined entirely to water (oceans). Single cellular living beings gradually evolved into complex multi-cellular beings. This led to the branching of life into plant and animal forms.

Gradually, there was division of work within the living body, with different organs doing different work to make the body more fit to survive.

Life forms took up strange and exotic shapes. Some living beings moved out of the oceans onto land. The scenario was quite insecure at that time. Life was nasty, brutish and short. In order to survive, living beings had to be fit for fight or for flight. Since the environment was different at different places, there evolved a lot of variations among living beings. Development of organs, like limbs to move, and body systems (like the digestive and circulatory systems etc.) were all evolutionary developments, provoked by the body to occur through the force of stress, in order to make the body more fit for survival.

In other words, it was stress that was shaping the body according to the environment so that the body was in a more favourable position for survival.

Stress always was and still is vital for our survival.

Since stress is a vital force of our life system, inherited through millions of years of evolution, we need not make any effort to get rid of stress, because such an attempt would be futile. Till we are alive, there would always be a stress factor ingrained in our body system. In fact, it is essential for our life. What is required is that the stress should be positive, conducive to our survival. It should not be negative, which is harmful for us. This is what is known as Stress Management – to manage our stress so that it helps us, but does not harm us.

In the next chapter, we will discuss how stress changed not only the body of living beings, but how it has also influenced our psychology.

■■

Development of the Human Psyche

Development of different organs in the body was simultaneously accompanied by the development of various body systems. At the same time, there developed a rudimentary nervous system to maintain co-ordination between different organs and body systems. The development of the nervous system was simultaneously being responded to by gradual development of various sensory organs. The body needed such communication and co-ordination systems for survival.

After development of the senses of perception (touch, vision, taste, smell, hearing) followed the development of memory. The body needed to retain past experiences. This was the beginning of the development of the brain. The elementary sensory system developed in the spinal chord and culminated in the development of the brain. Thus, the development of the brain was a requirement of the body, for the body was triggered by the survival instinct and driven by the force of stress.

With the development of memory the sense of co-relation and logic came about. The body needed to make sense out of what the memory retained or what the body perceived. And finally was developed the unique faculty of creativity in the human brain, a faculty that made man the fittest animal for survival, and gave him supreme power on earth over all other living beings.

The most developed living being, the human being, had in the process begun thinking. The earliest human beings with such intelligence are supposed to have existed some four million years ago. Thus, the process of evolution took almost six billion years to make us what we are today.

> *Stress is not something that has come up recently. It has always existed.*

Further, development of the mind and its related faculties (emotions and psychology) was also driven by stress. It must be remembered that stress is not something connected only with the mind. It is related to the body as well as the mind. In fact, there is no difference between the body and the mind in the sense that the brain is as much a part of the body as any other organ, with the primary function to help the body in its struggle for survival. Stress acts on the mind as well as the body in a co-ordinated way.

The Brain Reigns Supreme

As intelligence and consciousness about life and its environment developed, the survival instinct became the basic criterion of human perception. At this stage, something unique happened to human beings. This was the supremacy of the brain over the body. The brain, which had developed after a long process of evolution as an organ of the body meant to help the body in its struggle for survival, not only became independent in decision-making but also overwhelmed the body. It was the brain that was now deciding how the body should function, and the body was reacting to the thinking of the brain.

Thus, the functioning of the human body became, to a large extent, dependent on the way the human brain operated.

However, since the brain is nevertheless a body organ, and depends on the other organs of the body for sustenance, there is still a duality in functioning. This duality may be co-operative as well as contradictory. When the body and the brain function in mutual co-ordination, as friends, both benefit. However, if the brain functions independent of the interests of the body, both suffer. It is the creative part of the human brain's functioning that often leads to man developing a system of thought that is really not in the interest of man's body.

Because of a much better thinking apparatus, man was able to concentrate on more and more thoughts about his survival. Fears and emotions arose out of man's consciousness and apprehension of his own chances of survival in a world that was then mysterious and unknown to him. And there was death, which seemed so inexplicable and yet so certain, so inevitable. The feeling of insecurity and a concomitant instinct to survive fundamentally moulded not only our physical bearing and behaviour but also our entire psychology. Our fears and desires, likes and dislikes, in fact all our emotions, have their roots in that primeval spirit.

It must always be remembered that among all living beings, the ancestors of man were some of the physically weakest creatures. They did not have the horns of a bull, the ferocity of the tiger or the sting of a bee. They did not have anything like claws, fangs and tusks or superior physical strength. Without their intelligence, they were singularly unfit to survive. There were a large number of factors for man to be afraid of. That was the reason for such an extraordinary development of the human mind.

> *Fear was the most predominant feature of the human psyche. It still is.*

Threat and Survival

We still evaluate every signal that we receive from a threat percept. We categorise every stimulus fundamentally as either negative or positive, depending on whether it is favourable to our existence or against it. Further, emotions and feelings like love/hate, like/dislike, pity/apathy, attraction/aversion, etc. are all offshoots (secondary feelings) of the primary division of the stimuli into positive or negative categories.

Not only do we classify each stimulus into these two basic categories, as creative people we also have the unique capacity to create and invent threats where none exist. This is what makes the human psyche very complex. What scenarios one mind has invented, the other person cannot even imagine. The mind is capable of inventing its own set of expectations, interpretations and conclusions, which may not always have any relevance with reality. This is what is known as the emotional dimension of human beings. We will deal with the subject in more detail in a later chapter.

It is enough to clarify here that the survival instinct has its own threat percept. Everyone has his own threat percept, and a different threshold level for the threat percept. Different people view the same situation differently. Not everyone would take the same situation as a threat even if there were a potential for threat in that situation. And even if there were a certainty of threat for everyone in a situation, different people would assess the threat at different levels of scare. Some people get scared very easily; others take a situation as threatening only when the threat is actually very serious. This can also be understood as the threshold level of the survival instinct for categorisation of stimuli into the negative category.

While the survival instinct classifies all external objects, actions and other stimuli into positive and negative categories, the stress factor, innate in all living beings, compels us to take protective action in all cases of negative stimuli. This is to say that when our survival is threatened, or perceived to be under threat, the survival instinct activates stress in us. It is an inbuilt mechanism in us, whereby the body and the mind go into action, without our conscious knowledge or volition, to protect us from what is perceived as a threat, and by methods that the body has been conditioned to adopt over millions of years of evolution. It works automatically.

We cannot stop the body from functioning in the way it triggers stress, but we can certainly restrain it from becoming a problem for itself. In the next chapter we will discuss how stress is generated and how it actually works in our body system.

■■

How Stress is Generated

We have briefly discussed the process of evolution, how the survival instinct has used the force of stress to change and adapt our body to suit the environment in the struggle for survival, and how this process has led to the development of not only our body but also our mind.

Over the course of millions of years that this process of evolution has taken place, we have been conditioned to feel safe and comfortable within certain limited physical and psychological parameters. These are safety boundaries for our body and our mind, as perceived by the survival instinct. We can also call them our psychosomatic paradigms. Whenever these limits or parameters are transgressed, whether by the body or by the mind, the paradigm is violated, and the stress factor becomes active in a protective manner.

Anything that is beyond our comprehension (outside our parameters) affects us adversely. Enigmas seem to attack us. We are not comfortable with the mysterious and the unknown. Such things make us feel insecure. The instinct to survive makes it necessary for man to find solutions to such factors because without explanations he cannot come to terms with his own existence and his surroundings.

The entire development of human thought, the sciences and the arts has been, directly or indirectly, an endeavour to find answers to these questions. When we do not have an explanation, or when we perceive the explanation as negative, we feel threatened. And when we feel threatened, the stress factor comes into play, activating the mind, to devise means to help us overcome the perceived threat. Because that is what the stress factor has done for over a million years in our development, and has made us not only survive but also evolve into what we are today.

> *The mind and the body work on established patterns and paradigms.*

Paradigms, or limitations, can be of the body as well as of the mind. In order to understand this more clearly, we will examine certain illustrations of the paradigms of the body and then of the mind.

Paradigms of the Body

There are a large number of physical factors in our environment. Consider temperature, for example. You may not survive at freezing temperatures without protective clothing or external heat. On the higher side, you also cannot survive in the open at temperatures beyond 50°C. Whereas the gamut of the temperature zone begins from –273°C and may go as high as millions of Celsius, we can survive only within a very limited temperature zone.

Further, we are comfortable only within even a still more limited temperature zone, say between 15°C and 25°C. If it becomes somewhat warmer, or even somewhat cooler, our body feels threatened and signals that the environment (temperature) is not conducive to our survival, and automatically starts taking remedial action. This is the generation of active stress.

For example, if it is getting warm, we involuntarily start sweating; we unknowingly open our collars and look for air. If it gets colder, we fold our hands and squeeze ourselves to conserve heat. If these measures do not solve the problem, the body gives a message to the brain to undertake more positive steps. The brain switches off from the immediate task on hand and starts thinking about this new problem, and decides upon some action (like switching on/off the air-conditioner etc.). Once the problem has been attended to, stress again becomes dormant, and mind can go back to resume the task that was interrupted.

This is because during the millions of years of evolution, the body has been conditioned to survive within a very limited temperature zone, and the slightest indication of going out of this zone triggers the stress to take remedial action against what is perceived as a life-threatening situation. That is a physical paradigm of the body.

This paradigm is inbuilt in the body and is ingrained in our nervous system. We do not have to take conscious decisions about it. It works automatically. The moment we touch a very hot object, we jump away from it, and think later about what happened. In fact, it is so deeply inbuilt that we have no choice but to involuntarily make efforts to escape from such life-threatening situations. Thus, we have been given a body that is already preconditioned with certain limitations and physical attributes that can be called the paradigms of the body.

Similarly, we are comfortable within certain fixed limits of all other physical factors, like humidity, light, noise levels etc. The slightest deviation from these parameters activates the stress factor. These are the limitations of our body, or physical paradigms.

Paradigms of the Mind

Just as our body is preconditioned with certain attributes, so is our mind. This is so because the development of brain was a very gradual process, which took place along with, and in co-ordination with, the development of body.

The fundamental attributes of the way in which intellect operates are:

- ❑ Intellect should know what is going on (understand all the stimuli being received).
- ❑ It should be possible to categorise the stimuli into positive or negative categories.

- If a stimulus is in the negative category, there should be some solution to what is now being categorised as a threat.

The mind works continuously and keeps taking decisions on the above pattern without our being conscious of it. This is the paradigm of the mind. If the intellect is not able to close this operation for each stimulus with a conclusion that there is no threat, the situation is automatically classified as a threat and stress is generated to take corrective action. That is why the functioning of the mind plays a key role in generation as well as in management of stress.

Many of our problems are usually only in the mind. We have problems because we are not able to adjust to, or accept, things we do not like, or understand or feel apprehensive about. Strange things also threaten us. The problems are there only because things are often not as we would like them to be. It is a problem only because we want the situation to be otherwise. Had we not wanted it to be otherwise, it would not have been a problem in the first place.

But once we get a proper explanation, and find that there is no threat, we are relaxed. Even if the situation requires that we alter our parameters, we take a little time in adapting to the new situation, and then we are at ease. Till we do not have the explanation, confusion and conflict (apprehension) remain in our mind, and stress is exerted to find the answers and solutions for what our survival instinct treats as a life-threatening situation.

Continuing with the example of the problem of temperature discussed above, suppose the rise in temperature was due to failure of the air-conditioner, or power breakdown. We will make all attempts to understand the cause of the problem and likely time by which situation will be restored. Till the situation is uncertain, we remain under stress. But once we are told that help is on the way, our mind is eased.

Now let us see a few other illustrations of the paradigms of our mind:

- ❑ You hear a loud noise outside the window. You immediately want to know what has happened.
- ❑ You are walking on a street alone at night, and you see three men in a dark corner. You feel a sense of disquiet, if not fear.
- ❑ Your subordinate does not wish you 'Good Morning' one day. You are enraged.
- ❑ Your plane is delayed. You feel disgusted.
- ❑ Your son yells at you. You are annoyed.

What has happened? Why do you feel curious, angry, disturbed or annoyed when faced with such situations? Because certain things have happened for which you were not prepared for, or were not accustomed to. That is to say, you have been taken to an unknown territory, and since you do not know where this road is going to lead you to, you are in a state of conflict and confusion. These are cases of breach of paradigm of the mind, and stress is generated to compel the mind to find solutions for such situations.

This happens because the brain creates impressions out of the external signals it receives called perception. What we see with our eyes is a sight, a picture. The message that we infer from this picture is our perception. Our perception is formed by not only the sight but also by memories of events associated with similar sights, and is imbued with imagination. Thus, our perception is guided by our own knowledge and experience, with what we are accustomed to. It is conditioned.

Over the centuries, our mind also, like our body, has become accustomed to certain set behavioural patterns, certain customs and social norms. This is also known as the culture of society. These are the mental patterns, or paradigms of the mind. We are comfortable within these patterns. We feel safe when these established norms are followed. When these norms are violated, we may feel threatened, and thus uncomfortable. Our survival instinct classifies each sound, sight and gesture between the positive and the negative categories. Anything that is unknown and unexplained can be categorised as potentially dangerous. Till we do not resolve that there is no cause of danger, the stress factor remains active in us. We need answers for this breach of paradigm.

We can have the following answers to the above-mentioned situations:

- The loud noise was nothing but the bursting of a tyre of a scooter. When you looked out of the window, not only was your fear set at rest, but you were also amused to see a person dragging the scooter.
- The people you saw were friendly neighbours. You realised this when you got somewhat closer. Your fear changed into happiness.
- Your subordinate's son had met with an accident that very morning and so he was very disturbed. Once you came to know of this fact, you were sympathetic towards him, not annoyed.
- The plane was delayed because of a bomb scare. You felt happy that you were not on the plane.
- Your son has not been included in the school's cricket team. He is irritated. You come to know of this later, and encourage him to keep trying. The relationship is unaffected and amicable.

In all the above situations, it was ignorance about the full facts of the case, leading to imagination of negative (life-threatening) consequences that was the cause of the whole problem. The sensory organs of perception could collect only a fraction of the truth, or rather one aspect of the truth. What was not known was also classified in the negative category, as an apprehension, due to the creative faculty of the human mind.

Therefore, equipped with only part of the facts and supplemented with apprehensions about what was unknown, the survival instinct lost no time in concluding from the few available facts that there was a threat, and thus generated stress. This is partly due to the fact that unless we consciously make efforts to raise the threshold level of the survival instinct, it would lose no time in jumping to such conclusions, because the survival instinct is protective by nature and is designed to take such decisions quickly and on the safer side. Thus, unknown things are potential dangers in the human perception. However, once the truth is known, and there appears to be no danger, the stress level goes down. This takes time.

Changes in patterns take time for adaptation.
Till then there is confusion and conflict.

Once you know the reasons, you become comfortable. You find that none of the above-mentioned situations is a threat. Your stress subsides. It takes time to get the answers and to accept the facts. Even if the facts are not very pleasing, at least you know them. There is nothing more worrisome than being in the dark. Of course, you would take time to accept and adapt yourself to the new conditions, but you would not be under any stress or tension.

Crossing the Barriers

We all have a certain physical and mental capacity for work and endurance. This is also a paradigm. When we are made to do, or endure, beyond our capability, the paradigm is broken, and we become tense. Stress can get triggered when we are trying to attempt something beyond our capacity, either physically or mentally.

Because such situations are rare and we are not accustomed to such situations, we fear failure to accomplish the task we have undertaken. And failure is a life-threatening situation according to our survival instinct. Therefore, overexertion can also lead to stress.

Such situations can be:

- ❑ You are made to wait for three hours to get an appointment with the doctor.
- ❑ You have to stand in queue for two hours to get a ticket.
- ❑ There is an indefinite power cut during summers.
- ❑ Your boss wants you to complete the project report within 20 minutes.

Torments, physical or mental, especially when indefinite in periodicity, can cause severe stress. Many such situations demand a capability or endurance that may be beyond you. Commuters in cities who have to daily undergo harassing journeys by train or bus everyday are under severe stress. This is the reason that such groups are very volatile and resort to violent agitations quickly. When you have to suffer such situations, you undergo stress.

■■

Common Causes of Stress

We all know what we worry about; therefore, this needs no elaboration. We all have our own fears and the list would be endless.

Some of the common reasons affecting most of us are worry and fear regarding:

- ❑ Career or business
- ❑ Finance
- ❑ Health of family members or self
- ❑ Relationships
- ❑ Prestige
- ❑ Fear of ignominy or failure

Other factors that can cause stress are:

- ❑ Suppressed anger
- ❑ Frustration
- ❑ Boredom
- ❑ Despair and hopelessness
- ❑ Loss of status

It is important that we know what the cause of our stress is. We will discuss this subject in greater detail in another chapter.

It is important to understand that our body and our thinking have been conditioned over millions of years of evolution, and we are today bound by such conditioning. We do not have much choice about it. Our body and mind will involuntarily react on certain set patterns. Even without our knowing, our survival instinct will classify certain situations as life-threatening, and generate stress as a survival mechanism, whether we like it or not.

This is the reason why I say that no living person can be totally without stress. Stress would be there within us most of the time. However, it is very important to know when negative stress has gone too far and begun hurting instead of protecting us, and when this is known, we must act to control stress. Therefore, it becomes very important to know the symptoms of stress.

■■

Symptoms of Stress

Before discussing stress any further, it is necessary to have a brief glance over the symptoms and signals of negative stress. The problem with stress is that it is often diagnosed much after it has advanced fairly deeply into our system.

The most intriguing thing about stress is that:

> *You may not be aware*
> *that you are under stress!*

However, there are certain visible and perceptible early signals of negative stress that can be known. Check for the under-mentioned symptoms:

- **Constant Fatigue and General Lack of Energy**

  Constant fatigue does not mean feeling tired after you have done really strenuous exercise/work, or when you are otherwise sick or recuperating from sickness. It pertains to the feeling of tiredness, exhaustion and lethargy without any apparent reason.

- ❑ Do you constantly feel tired, listless and without energy right in the morning, and without being otherwise ill?
- ❑ Do you feel worn-out by midday?
- ❑ Do you often tell yourself that if you could have a little more rest you would feel fine?

If the answer is yes, you may be under stress. Do not delude yourself by making excuses such as:

- ❑ "I am not a child any more. I am past 45."
- ❑ "It is a matter of age."
- ❑ "I have been working hard this week."

Remember, the human body is built to remain energetic till a very ripe age. Merely taking more rest would not help. Check with your physician if there is any medical problem. If there is none, you may be under stress.

- **Insomnia and Drowsiness**

  If you constantly feel that you need more sleep, but cannot sleep, it may be due to stress. The worst thing about insomnia is that it is not only an effect of stress but also a cause of stress. Lack of sleep may be due to stress and may also lead to further stress.

If you do not get enough sleep, at least do not lose sleep worrying about it! Your body may not be in need of more sleep. Remember, unless you are otherwise sick, an average of about six hours' sleep is enough for a healthy person.

Check if some changes in your sleeping pattern, or in your bedroom, are making an improvement in your sleeping habits. Early to bed and early to rise is still the key to good health. If you still sleep less, do not worry. Get out of bed and get on with work. The body will take its own natural course.

Your posture while sleeping is also very important. Sleeping straight and flat on the back (on a hard bed, with a very shallow pillow) gives you the most relaxed sleep, as you are able to have maximum free inhalation, and the intake of oxygen is thereby maximised. Sleeping on the tummy is the worst thing to do. It restricts breathing and is bad for digestion also.

- **Stiff Neck and Backache**

❑ Do you often have backache and the doctor tells you there is nothing wrong? Did he not tell you about stress?

❑ Rotate your neck and try to see an object directly at your back from both the sides. If you are unable to comfortably rotate the neck, and the neck bones make crackling sounds, it may be due to spondylosis. This is a sure sign of stress. To a very large extent, spondylosis is due to stress, and when you suffer from it, you feel dizzy and feel pain around the chest, as if you are going to have a heart attack. This requires prompt attention on the lines prescribed in this book.

These are very critical symptoms of stress, and should not be ignored.

Some other symptoms:

- ❑ Lack of concentration
- ❑ Forgetfulness
- ❑ Indifferent mood
- ❑ Irritability
- ❑ Desire to be left alone
- ❑ Indigestion and loss of appetite
- ❑ Weight loss or weight gain
- ❑ Frequent headaches

The above symptoms should not be neglected if they affect you frequently and for a long duration of time. They should not be wished away as a mere passing phase. It is recommended that you have a medical check-up. Unless these symptoms are due to any specific medical problem, they are likely to be due to accumulated stress.

■■

Silent Killer of the Modern Age

We have discussed how stress is generated and what the symptoms of negative stress are. It is essential that we understand how negative stress affects our body.

During the course of evolution, as the body developed complex organs and body systems, there also developed internal systems of regulation and coordination between different systems. The human body maintains coordination between various systems, and regulates them as well through the endocrine system. The endocrine system can be understood as the system of hormones. Hormones are chemicals secreted into the blood by the endocrine glands of the body. These hormones influence the operations of all the body's tissues and organ systems. Different types of endocrine glands secrete different hormones for different functions.

The two fundamental needs of any living being for survival are sustenance and protection. Sustenance is provision of food, water, air and the like. Protection means shelter from threats of the external environment. The body needs to do some activity to fulfil these two primary needs. And for performing any activity, the body requires energy and strength. Assimilation, retention and dissipation of energy and strength is done in the body by a complex network of body systems, and regulated by hormones. The hormone that regulates and controls this function is called adrenaline. When we need extra energy and extra strength, the body generates adrenaline to activate the systems that lead to generation of this extra strength and energy.

For millions of years, the threats that the body faced were physical or material in nature. Man had to fight or flee for safety, and both these activities needed strength and energy. Over thousands of years, the human body has countered external threats by generating adrenaline. This is, again, a paradigm of the body mechanism.

> *The fundamental reaction of the body is still primitive. It is an immediate response to a perceived danger.*

The body knows that generating adrenaline is the best way to overcome a threat to survival. The body still reacts in the same way towards anything it perceives as a threat, that is, by rushing adrenaline.

Adrenaline has the following effects on your system:

- ❑ Heart rate and blood pressure increase.
- ❑ Blood is redirected to the large muscle groups to give you extra strength and energy.
- ❑ Blood supply to other systems is reduced. Consequently, the other systems (like the digestive and immune systems) become inactive in order to conserve energy.
- ❑ The mind becomes hyperactive and searches for areas of danger.
- ❑ Emotions like fear, anger, aggression, nervousness and anxiety grip you.

We must know that all our organs function through muscles. These need energy for functioning, which is supplied through blood. Since blood in the body is a limited quantity, the mind rushes the blood more to those organs that are more in need of energy at a particular time. If more blood is supplied to the larger muscles of hands and legs, then smaller muscles of organs like the stomach and intestine etc. are temporarily deprived of blood, and hence they become temporarily inactive and dormant.

This state of extra adrenaline cannot continue for long without having damaging effects. The rush of adrenaline also leads to the following adverse effects:

- ❑ Burning up of your body resources leads to fatigue.
- ❑ Inactivity of other systems leads to their disorder.
- ❑ The immune cells are no longer able to pass through the capillary walls of the blood vessels. This inhibits their ability to destroy and remove harmful bacteria from the body. The immune system is thereby adversely affected.
- ❑ Fatigue of the mind due to constant alertness leads to loss of concentration and temporary forgetfulness.
- ❑ You suffer from sleep disorders.
- ❑ Emotions become negative. You feel unhappy, and tend to become asocial.

The rushing of adrenaline was good in primitive times when any danger required an immediate physical response, and lasted for short durations of time. (How long can the danger of confronting a lion last? There has to be a resolution, one way or the other, within a few minutes!) However, the dangers of today are not physical in nature and they are of longer durations. Today if you have a boss who makes your life miserable, you may have to suffer because of him for years together, only to be replaced by another senile one. The problem just refuses to vanish. This persistence of the problem creates a dangerous situation.

Threat and Perception

However, a fundamental change has taken place in the environment of human beings over the past few hundred years, particularly in the past one hundred years. That is, in what we view as a threat percept. At this stage, we must differentiate between a *threat* and a *threat percept.*

A threat is a real and tangible danger. Confronting a tiger in a forest is a real danger. Being without water or food in the middle of a desert is another real danger. Being trapped in a burning house is a threat to life. A confirmed report that one is suffering from blood cancer is also a real threat. These are real threats to the further continuance of the life of your body that can be substantiated, verified and proved by any external agency. There would be no difference of opinion on such issues.

However, *threat percept is our assessment of a situation as a threat.* It is a sort of individual opinion of a person, or group of persons. It is not something that is physically tangible, but something that the individual thinks is a threat. It is his perception or view of a situation as a threat. Since this is primarily a matter of the mind of an individual, there may be differences of opinion about it, because different people would view a situation differently. Since it is a matter of thought, it is not always related to the possibility of a physical danger to the body. It may be related to some other facet of the mind, like emotions. This is what makes a fundamental difference between how humans react to threats today, as compared to how they reacted some 20,000 years ago.

For six billion years, the threat to a living being was danger to his body. It was pure physical damage to the body that the survival instinct tried to assiduously avoid, resist and overcome. When human beings first began walking the plains of the Rift Valley (present-day Ethiopia in Africa), some four million years ago, the threats were the same. Primitive man was just an intelligent animal, with the same needs and the same fears.

In fact, because man was physically weaker than other animals, it was his intellect that became his tool for survival. This only led to man having a much lower threshold level for threat percept. He was more easily frightened. He could anticipate, comprehend and even imagine fears more easily than other animals.

This continued till a few thousand years ago, when concepts of civilisation began developing. Civilised living began changing the social norms of relationships. This led to certain fundamental changes in man's understanding of his identity. As life became more secure, physical threats were supplemented and supplanted with threats of the mind. The pace of civilised behaviour was much faster in the past hundred years.

Today we simply cannot imagine how our ancestors must have lived only a couple of thousand years ago. And they had lived like that for over four million years. We cannot imagine what their challenges, their thoughts and their emotions must have been. The entire mindset of man has changed over the past few centuries. This change has been too fast.

Most threats that we face today are not direct physical threats. Present-day threats pertain to our job, our finances, or our relationships. These factors are related more to our emotions than to our body. We do not need physical effort to counter these problems. However, a few hundred years is too short a time for body systems to change their fundamental behaviour. Whereas our intellect has transformed, the body continues to be the same and still reacts to each threat as it did for the past millions of years – by activating adrenaline.

Stress Erodes the Immune System

Hormonal imbalance caused by stress seriously affects the regulating mechanism of the systems of the body. Excess release of adrenaline puts the entire system of the body into overdrive. Some organs become hyperactive at the cost of other systems. For example, excess secretion of gastric juices can cause ulcers. Similarly, unnecessary pumping of extra blood causing a higher pulse rate leads to circulatory disorders like high blood pressure. When the body is full of adrenaline its metabolism is speeded up, consuming more of the body's resources and producing more waste and toxins that will need to be removed.

The problem is that in modern society the natural process is not taking place to burn up the excess adrenaline and remove the extra toxins from the system. Over a period of time, the worst effect the hormonal imbalance does is to our immune system. It makes us weak internally, and we become vulnerable to several physical disorders.

This is why stress has been called a silent killer.

> *Physical factors can also trigger stress in the mind.*

Stress is not something exclusively mental in nature. It is perhaps this dimension that distinguishes stress from tension, which is attributed mainly to the state of mind. Stress can be of the body also, or it can be of both. In fact, it works both ways. If our mind is in trouble, it affects the body and if the body is in any physical stress, it gives distress signals to the mind looking for rescue and generates stress in the mind also. If there is no solution to the problems either of the body or the mind, a vicious cycle starts. Thus, the problem of the mind affects the body, and the problem of the body affects the mind. It is this vicious cycle that is most dangerous.

> *Cause and effect of stress reinforce one and the other. Physical and mental stress go hand in hand, feeding each other in a vicious cycle.*

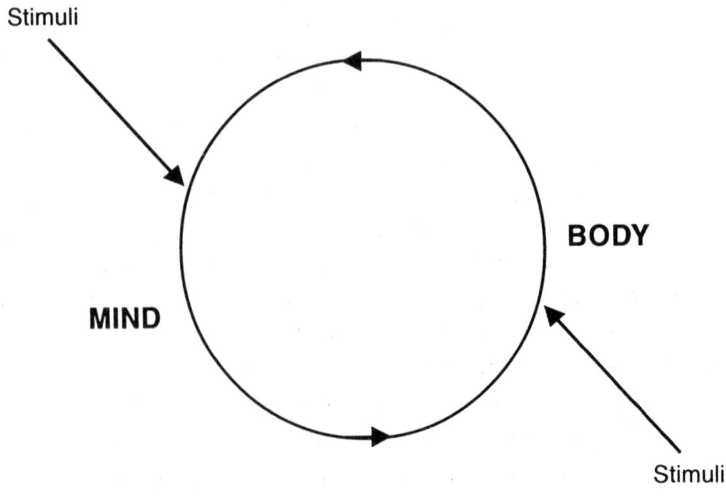

In today's life, there can hardly be a situation when we are not subjected to stresses of the body or the mind from time to time. We all face some stress all the time. Such stresses will only increase in complexity as we make further progress in civilization. In fact, just as body developed due to stress, similarly societies and civilizations develop due to stress. It is a part of the process of development, and hence unavoidable. These stresses can never be avoided.

The question is: *What do we do? This vicious cycle has to be broken.*

While we perhaps cannot avoid factors that generate stress from affecting us, we can surely isolate and localise these factors and prevent them from starting the vicious cycle. If you are able to break this vicious cycle, then you have succeeded in controlling the negative stress.

For doing this:

You have to change the way you think and live!

■■

Four Components of Human Personality

We have by now discussed how stress came into being as an integral part of our body's mechanism, how stress is triggered, and how it adversely affects us.

We know that we cannot avoid stress. But we should be able to manage it in such a way that while the positive stress keeps helping us in our endeavour for survival, its negative effects do not cause us any harm. For this, we have to break the vicious cycle of stress.

How do we break the vicious cycle? For this, it is necessary that we understand the four components of human personality.

Living beings first came up as physical beings, that is, living beings with a body. Development of the brain, or the intellect, came later. With intellect came emotions, and humans finally developed a spiritual aspect. We all have these four components in our psychosomatic system; that is to say, body, intellect, emotions and spirituality are the four components of human personality. Stress is related to all the four, and when we want to control stress we have to deal with it in all the four aspects.

We will discuss these four dimensions of the human personality, and how to manage stress in each of its four facets or components, in the same order as we humans have developed.

This can also be called the:

4-Lane Road to Stress Management

- Body
- Intellect
- Emotions
- Spirituality

I term this a four-lane road because the road is one, and all these four components are integral to the road. They are interlinked. They go together. However, each one leads to the same destination. This does not mean that if you follow any of these four lanes you would be able to control stress. This implies that if you take care of only one or two of these dimensions and ignore the others, stress would take the other lane and go ahead to affect you. Thus, stress has to be dealt with in all four of its components.

There are many exponents of stress management today, who are masters of one of these four lanes. They overemphasise one dimension and ignore the others. This leaves a lot of room for stress to strike. Stress has to be dealt with in all four aspects. We will deal with these four in the subsequent chapters.

■■

STRESS MANAGEMENT

LANE I

The Body

We humans began our life form as a body, and we still are primarily a physical being. Without this body we are nowhere. Taking care of this body is of prime importance to us. There are many exponents and gurus of stress management who concentrate only on the emotional and spiritual methods of tackling stress. Whereas these aspects are also very important (and we would also be dealing with them later), I would like to emphasise that if we do not take care of the body, we can never be free of the ill effects of negative stress that always keep affecting us.

In fact, dealing with stress only at the emotional or spiritual level may give a false sense of well-being. You may be under the impression that you are free of stress, while the negative effects of stress may be silently damaging your health, without your knowing this till you perceive its visible symptoms. By then, much damage has already been done.

Taking good care of our health is of prime importance at all times. Your slogan should be: *I shall stay healthy.*

Remember – only a healthy body can continue to fight. Efforts to remain healthy not only keep you fit but also break the vicious circle of stress. For this you have to correct your lifestyle.

The three major components to stay healthy are: Diet, Exercise and Relaxation.

Diet

It has been truly said that *you are what you eat.* Your diet should be balanced and nutritious. Excessive consumption of any one type of food is not good. Unless your doctor has restricted certain foods for medical reasons, all foods – including fats and oils – taken in moderation are good for you. Special attention should be given to breakfast, which should be the most nutritious meal of the day. Lunch should be moderate. And dinner should always be light.

There is an entire range of literature available on health-benefiting foods, and one should make it a point to read some of these books. It would be out of place to go into specifics of the same here. However, certain bare essentials need to be mentioned.

The following foods are recommended, especially for breakfast:

- **Seasonal fruits** that provide essential vitamins and minerals (salts), which are necessary for vitality as well as for keeping the hormonal system in balance. It is not necessary to consume an excess quantity of fruits. Even a small quantity may be good enough. What is important is to eat a variety of fruits available in season, and to consume them regularly, even if in small quantities. Fruits and vegetables of bright red and yellow colour are particularly good. Green leafy vegetables are also very good.
- **Sprouts** of gram (*chana*) and lentils, particularly *moong*. These provide essential proteins as well as vitamins. Sprouted *menthi* is also good to control hypertension.
- **All milk products**, including *ghee* of cow's milk.
- **Garlic and ginger**. Garlic takes care of many problems like hypertension and cholesterol. Ginger too has many health benefits.
- **Soya**. This has several essential ingredients.
- **Water**. Take plenty of water. At least 12 glasses of water should be consumed in a day. Of these, three to four glasses (1.15 litres) should be taken within the first 20 minutes of waking up in the morning. It flushes out your entire system and is extremely good for health,

especially for those suffering from constipation and those wanting to reduce weight. Water also dissolves the toxins generated by the rush of adrenaline and thus removes them from the body.

Reduce Weight Safely

These days, obesity is becoming a serious problem. Many people are resorting to severe dieting to reduce weight. A little caution on the subject is necessary at this point.

If you are overweight, change the nature of your diet instead of skipping meals and starving yourself. In fact, starving to reduce weight is not good for health. It would be better to substitute oily and starchy foods with fruits, sprouts and vegetables, rather than to reduce the quantity of food. Starvation diets may have long-term adverse effects on health. Skipping breakfast to reduce weight is particularly damaging to health.

Doing regular exercise, along with a change in the nature of diet, is a much better option. In fact, no type of dieting has any meaning unless followed up with exercise.

It must also be remembered that the weight and shape of one's body to a large extent depend on genetic factors. You must accept what you have inherited. Rather than trying to drastically change that, it is better to concentrate on the functional aspects of the body. We should not be too concerned about the symmetry of our physique. Ultimately, health is more important than the shape of your body!

There is no alternative to exercise.
It is the best medicine.

Exercise should also be balanced and regular. The extent and pattern of exercise will depend on the age and physical condition of the person. If you have not been exercising regularly since long, do not start suddenly with a very vigorous schedule. Do not attempt to become a Premchand Degra or Arnold Schwarzeneggar in one day! You will end up with cramps, torn muscles, or even a fracture maybe. Begin gradually and increase the intensity slowly. People suffering from any type of disease should always consult a doctor before starting any exercise regimen. The fundamental purpose of exercise should be that all parts of the body, all joints and all muscles get some exercise.

If you have the facilities to play games, that is best because games not only provide you the required exercise but also give you a much-needed break from the routine. This breaks the vicious stress cycle both at the physical level as well as at the mental level, not to speak of the benefits that you get out of socialising on the sports field. However, if you do not have the opportunity, or cannot play games for other reasons, schedule a workout plan at home. Buy a stationary cycle and couple of light weights, and get started.

Some people have a casual walk in the morning in the name of exercise. Whereas something is always better than nothing, it must be remembered that walking alone is not enough. Walking is a very good exercise for older people, but not a complete exercise for younger people. If you are younger and only into walking, ensure you are into fast walking.

The exercise routine should have the following parts in the given sequence:

a) Gradual warming up and loosening of muscles and joints for about five minutes before starting any exercise is necessary. Stretch yourself at different angles, but do not stretch more than what you can with comfort. Avoid jerks at all costs. Sudden vigorous exercise may damage muscles and joints.

b) Aerobics should follow the warm up, so that each muscle gets sufficient quantity of blood, and the body is prepared for more vigorous exercises.

c) The vigorous part of the exercise for burning up calories (jogging, cycling or some fast sport) should be done after warm up and aerobics.

d) Use of light weights for toning up and strengthening muscles, joints and bones should be a part of the vigorous exercise. However, for those who have not been using weights, care should be taken that weights are very light and do not cause pain. Lifting very light weights more number of times is better than lifting a heavy weight once. The intention is not to build up muscles, but rather to tone them up. If it pains, reduce the weights, or give a break to this part of the exercise for a few days.

e) Then move into a gradual cool down and relaxation to keep the muscles loose and warm, otherwise you may have cramps and muscle stiffness after the vigorous exercises.

f) *Yoga* – this should be learnt from a competent trainer and initially practised under supervision only. Once you have learnt the various yogic *asanas*, you can do it alone. In case you have any medical problem, it would be necessary to consult your physician before starting.

g) Deep breathing exercises *(pranayama)* are very good. In fact, *prayanama,* if practised even for 10-15 minutes per day can do wonders to all aspects of your health. It should preferably be learnt from a good practitioner.

Certain very good CDs are now also available for imparting *yoga* instructions. These can be played on home computer/TV. These should be tried. However, there is nothing better than personal instruction from a *yoga* exponent in the beginning.

Important Things to Remember

- Exercise should start slowly and end slowly.
- Do not overexert. Stop short of palpitation or breathlessness.
- Relax after a workout. After 10 minutes of relaxation, you should feel recharged and refreshed. If you still

feel too tired and exhausted, you have exercised more than what your system can sustain. Reduce the level.

- Thirty minutes of exercise is the barest minimum. Cool down gradually.
- Any strenuous exercise should always be done on an empty stomach (at least two hours after having a meal).
- Too much water should not be taken before or even during exercise. However, in the summer months very small quantities of water with salt (preferably rock salt) should be taken during exercise if there is excess perspiration, as is likely in a warm climate, in order to avoid dehydration.
- The place where you exercise should neither be too cold nor too warm. It is essential that the body does not get exposed to cold during and immediately after the exercise. Such exposure can do much harm.
- It is essential that there is no sudden break during the exercise schedule. Keep away from telephones while exercising (attend to your phone calls later).
- Breathing should be deep and slow. Bear in mind that the lungs take time in utilising the oxygen you have inhaled. Retention of inhaled air for a couple of seconds gives the maximum utilisation of the oxygen that we inhale. Quick and shallow breaths only give an impression that we are taking more oxygen, whereas such breathing takes more time to provide the extra oxygen that we need when breathless.
- The place of exercise should be as free from pollution as possible. Those who walk or jog regularly on roads often do not realise that on account of heavy pollution, they are likely to inhale a lot of poisonous gases, which can do more harm than the accumulated benefits of the exercise.
- Wear loose clothes while exercising. A tracksuit is the best option.

You cannot avoid stress. But you can avoid the adverse effects of stress by keeping fit.

Benefits of Exercise

- It keeps your body fresh, fit and healthy.
- Exercise removes toxins generated due to the rush of adrenaline.
- Exercise consumes the excess adrenaline.
- It has a feel-good effect, which gives positive signals to our mind and increases our feeling of well-being.
- Exercise keeps the body in good shape, which increases the sense of self-esteem. People with a body in good shape are likely to have a higher level of self-esteem than those who have sloppy bodies. This increases the emotional or psychological strength of the person.
- A physically fit person is always in a better position to tackle his problems than one who is physically unfit.
- Exercise generates self-confidence and increases the threshold level of the survival instinct. A physically fit person is less likely to perceive minor problems as a threat compared to an unhealthy person. Thus, the generation of stress would not be as frequent as it would be in an unhealthy person. Therefore, he would not get into the stress cycle as easily as one who is unfit.
- During times of tension and stress, the exercise period affords a much-needed break from the vicious cycle of stress. If a person has a fitness routine of exercises in the morning and evening, even if for a short duration, then the body gets a break from the vicious cycle twice in every 24 hours. This is enough to relieve a person from the physical damage that is likely to take place when a person is under stress.

- Exercise forces the body to resume all normal activities. As stated earlier, when we are under stress, the normal function of the brain to maintain the balance between the different systems of the body gets affected. This leads to imbalance and lack of coordination between different systems. This is a major cause of several problems. However, when we exercise, our body is forced to resume normal functioning, and the system gets a break from all the stress.

> *Train your body and mind to relax.*

Relaxation is almost as important as exercising. However, in this context, relaxation does not mean merely resting. Relaxation certainly does not mean watching TV serials. (When we watch serials, we absorb the stresses of the characters of the serials as well. Then why take their problems into your mind?) We have to relax our body as well as our mind. Relaxation of the mind means giving your mind a brief period of thoughtlessness. This is known as meditation – a state of mind when there are no thoughts and the mind is in deep rest. This is nature's antidote to stress. Meditation requires training, however, and should be begun only under proper guidance. For this reason, we cannot explain this in further detail here.

> *Alcohol, cigarettes and drugs create an illusion of relaxation but, in reality, only suppress and thereby increase stress. Escapism does not help.*

Dangers of Tobacco

This is one of the greatest threats to your health. Tobacco acts slowly, but affects very deeply. It is much more addictive than alcohol and more dangerous to health. We all know that smoking or chewing tobacco can lead to cancer of the lungs, mouth and tongue, etc. Many people delude themselves by adopting a fatalistic attitude saying that if it is destined to be so, it will be so. What they do not realise is that whether tobacco causes cancer or not, it certainly saps your energy, makes you tired, raises your blood pressure and gives a false impression of revitalisation.

Thus, by eroding your stamina and power of resistance, tobacco not only reduces your lifespan but also affects the quality of life you lead, especially in your old age.

Tobacco is extremely difficult to give up because it causes serious withdrawal symptoms. The best method is to give it up suddenly. If you try to give it up by slowly reducing your intake, you may never succeed. Suddenly giving it up would no doubt cause withdrawal problems. Seek social support at such a time. Tell everyone that you have given up smoking to be healthy. Through autosuggestion and social approval you will be able to strengthen your resolve to quit. The withdrawal symptoms may last from 15 days to a couple of months. Be ready to bear that.

Soon, you will find so much extra energy and strength generated inside you that you will feel happy you have given up tobacco. Then there is no fear that you will go back to it. It is only the initial period of withdrawal that is difficult.

During my lectures on stress management, I always ask how many participants indulge in regular exercise. I find that not more than ten per cent of men and less than five per cent of women claim that they indulge in any type of exercise regularly. The non-exercisers come up with all sorts of reasons and excuses for not working out: they do not find time, their work itself is a form of exercise and exhausting and what not.

My answer to all these alibis is simple. If you wish to, go ahead and deceive everyone you like, but please do not deceive yourself. You can throw dust in anyone's eyes, but what is the point of throwing dust in your own eyes? Do not treat yourself like an enemy. Be your own friend.

As regards the issue of sparing time for exercises is concerned, if you start going to sleep early (instead of watching TV) you can get up early enough in the morning with sufficient time for exercise. It is only a question of priorities of life. Give highest priority to health and you will easily find the time.

Take care of your body. It is your own body, your own vehicle that will carry you on your journey of life. It is more important than your car, your cell phone, your house, all your assets and your ephemeral status.

Taking care of your body will certainly require your attention, conscious effort and time. But remember, if you ignore your health today, the time will come when your body begins creating problems. Then you will be wasting much more time and money on your health, and also suffer the fear of death, which can be extremely damaging.

So, take care. Now!

■■

Stress Management

Lane II

The Intellect

Earlier, we had discussed how the development of a complex body system was closely followed by the development of the central nervous system, which finally culminated in the development of the brain. The brain was an organ of the body, which evolved over a period of time so that the body was in a better position for survival.

Like any other body organ, the brain was not supposed to have an independent existence. But in the case of the highly developed brains of human beings, that is precisely what has happened: The brain has become the controller and master of the body. It can think on its own, and often makes the body act as it wants. The brain's power over the body has gone a bit too far, sometimes more than what is good for the body itself.

The problem is that the instinct for survival is so overwhelming in the human brain that it blows any threat percept totally out of proportion. The brain exaggerates problems and dwells over them for far too long than is necessary. The faculty of creativity in the human mind often clouds reality as well as rationality. Thus, reception of the signal of threat and pain itself becomes a major problem rather than an indicator of the problem.

When we are under tension due to any problem, the worst thing that we can do is to continuously worry about the problem. This is most harmful. The dread of fearsome but imaginary consequences so completely overwhelms us that we are neither able to analyse the exact magnitude of the problem, nor take rational decisions to overcome it. We keep thinking only about the problem and not about the solutions!

On the other hand, sometimes we begin avoiding the problem. We do not want to face the problem, and so do not want to even think about it, as if by ignoring it we will be able to avoid it. We start denying the very existence of the problem. By constant autosuggestion, we succeed in convincing ourselves that the problem does not exist. Unfortunately, such self-denial does not help because we have the problem at the back of our mind and keep worrying about it subconsciously.

Since our thoughts in such a situation have no proper direction, nor an action plan, we remain vague about the problem and bereft of a solution. This not only adds to our stress, but also seriously limits our capability to effectively deal with our problem(s). This happens because we do not train our mind to think positively. Like any other part of the body, the mind also needs training on the way of thinking. We cannot let the mind think in any way it likes. We have to control and discipline our intellect so that we are able to think in a way that is helpful, and not damaging to us.

When you are in a problem and tense because of that, follow the lane of intellect. What is required is that our thinking and outlook change from negative to positive. The most fundamental purpose of pursuing the Lane of Intellect in stress management is to:

Shift your focus from problems to solutions!

This path is to be followed by way of doing an intellectual exercise. Do this exercise by writing the various steps on paper. Why is writing it essential? Because only by thinking about it we cannot do this exercise. We are so overwhelmed by the emotions generated by our problems that we are never dispassionate about things that are likely to affect us. Hence, we fail to be rational in analysing our own problems. And the human mind is so creative that we are able to imagine problems that do not exist at all. However, when we start writing all that we think and feel, we are able to think more clearly and rationally. Writing helps in crystallising our own thoughts. Only then can we segregate the factual from the imaginary, the material from the emotional.

When you do this exercise for the first time, I recommend that you take the help of a friend. It may be difficult to do it alone. A friend can tender good advice, guide you in pinpointing the relevant issues, keep you focussed, and help you with good solutions, which you may not be able to think of yourself due to your mental commotion. In any case, a partner always acts as a sounding board. He echoes your own words, so that you listen to what you are saying. This helps in clearing your own thoughts.

However, it must be ensured that the friend should not be emotionally attached to you or your problem, because this has to be a cold intellectual exercise that you do, as if the problem that you are going to analyse is not your problem but someone else's.

Rather, treat this as a theoretical or hypothetical problem. For this reason, your spouse may not be the best person to be associated with in this exercise, as s/he would never be able to think dispassionately about your problems.

Step 1: Analyse the Nature of Your Problem

- ❑ Is the problem emotional (one of mind) or is it material?
- ❑ Is the problem conceptual or physical?

Remember, some of the biggest problems of our life are merely emotional in nature. Major conflicts and devastating wars that have taken place in this world have been fought for conceptual reasons, not material reasons. Alexander the Great left Macedonia to conquer the world, not because there was any shortage of food in his country, but because he had a concept in his mind to be the conqueror of the world. A thought, a conviction, an idea or an emotional urge can create havoc in the society. It always does. Whatever Hitler did was an outcome of his ideas that became his conviction and so an emotional necessity for him to do.

Why are there so many wars, bloodshed and conflicts because of religion? Has god told anyone to fight for his cause? Would god need human beings to fight for his cause? Is any god so weak and ineffective that he needs men to defend him? Has god told anyone to do such things on his behalf? Why do certain religions, even while saying that all are children of god, still believe in converting people to their own religion? Do they feel that god will be happy only if people have the stamp of a particular religion? Do they mean to say that their god is prejudiced and unfair? Are there many gods fighting for supremacy over earth?

These are very difficult and embarrassing questions that no one would like to answer. There can be no rational answers to these questions. The standard answer is that these are matters of trust and faith. (Hence, the term non-believer.) In fact, these are matters of concept or imagination. Religion is a concept, a thought. Yet, today it is the cause of many of the world's problems. Someone else not believing in the type of god you have been conditioned to believe in is an uncomfortable (life-threatening) situation! Hence the religious conflicts!

If someone deprives you of your money or causes you bodily harm, then it is a material problem. Something leading you to starvation, loss of shelter or clothing is a material problem.

But someone not showing respect to you, not appreciating your achievement, not accepting your point of view, not loving you... such situations are emotional in nature. Should we call them problems at all?

You feel comfortable in certain situations (the ones that you perceive are favourable to your survival) and uncomfortable in certain other situations (those that you perceive as threatening your survival). Therefore, you want situations to be comfortable to your existence. That is your concept. So, if the situation turns out to be otherwise, which is not to your liking, your survival instinct treats it as a life-threatening situation, and triggers stress. Even the most minor and harmless changes in the situation, which may have no actual element of threat, can also be categorised as a threat by our survival instinct.

Unfortunately, the survival instinct does not easily treat situations as neutral situations. It is always either for or against you.

Whereas material problems have a solution (the hungry man simply needs food), conceptual problems have no rational and amicable solutions, because you cannot reason out a solution to a problem that has its origins based not on reason but on imagination.

> *Conflicts created out of imagination cannot be solved by reason, unless you realise that the nature of the problem is conceptual, not material.*

In emotional or conceptual conflicts, one party always wants the other party to surrender their concept in favour of the former's concept (accept my god and give up your god!). Since there is no control over imagination, there are no solutions to conceptual conflicts, like those related to religion.

When you are beset with tension, first analyse the nature of your problem. Once you have come to the answer to this first question, regarding whether the problem has any material basis or is only conceptual in nature, you will yourself come to the conclusion about how much significance it deserves. You will realise whether the problem is only in your mind, or it has a solid basis.

One is not saying that emotions do not matter. They do matter. Situations that attack our sense of pride, love, affection, justice, status, ego and the like do matter in life. Acknowledge these emotions, do not deny them, but always analyse them. The question is not whether it is an emotional issue or not. The question is, to what extent would you like such emotional issues to affect your life.

Later in this book, we will discuss in more detail how to manage our emotions. Here, suffice it to say that you should be very clear in your own mind about the nature of your problem, while doing this exercise. Then you have to ask yourself the following question:

Do you want emotions and imaginary concepts to spoil your health, affect your working and deprive you of your happiness?

Be your friend:

> *Do not let imaginary and emotional issues spoil your life.*

Emotions like anger, envy and vengeance, thoughts about settling scores and the like are the root cause of all your problems and unhappiness. Emotional problems often lead to real material problems also. Would you like imaginary problems to turn into real problems? The answer depends on whether you are being your own friend or your own enemy. If you let your own thinking cause you grief and stress, then you are not being your friend.

Step II: Analyse the Precise Cause of Your Stress

After coming to a definite conclusion about whether your tension is emotional or material, the next step is to identify the reason or cause of the tension. The objective of this part of the exercise is to pinpoint the exact factor. List all the possible causes that you can think of, and then take the help of your friend in pinpointing the real cause. The reason may be a person or a set of circumstances. And that person may even be YOU! And the set of circumstances may be of your own making! Do not be untruthful to yourself. Analyse to what extent you were the cause of the problem. There is no point blaming only others. Go to the bottom of the cause.

Think, who started the whole thing? Is there someone responsible for this situation or is it because of certain unavoidable circumstances?

Such in-depth analyses would help you in identifying the root cause of the problem, hence you would know where to look for solutions as well.

At this stage if you come to the conclusion that the problem confronting you is only conceptual in nature (problem of the mind) and that no particular person is responsible, then you should accept that no further action is required on the subject, and as such there is no reason to further waste your time or thoughts worrying about it. The exercise should end at this stage.

If you find that the problem is emotional and that someone (including you) is the cause, then it needs emotional treatment. This has been discussed in greater detail in the next chapter.

Step III: Write Down the Consequences

If the problem is genuine and not imaginary (as analysed in Step I) and you know the precise cause of the problem (as analysed in Step II) you must also know what this problem is going to lead you to. Where would it end? Now list the consequences you can think of. A problem is a problem only if it has some adverse consequences. You should know exactly what adverse consequences the problem is likely to have. When listing the possible consequences, take care that you:

> *Focus on the immediate issues,*
> *not what will happen after 10 years!*

With our fertile and extremely creative mind, we are not only able to create problems where none exist, but we are also able to blow up the possible consequences far out of proportion. We imagine things that have a remote chance of happening 10 to 15 years from now. We fear such things also and worry about them. While taking care of the future is also important, we should not lose sight of the immediate issues. In any case, there is a lot of difference between planning for the future and worrying about the future.

While taking care to maintain focus on the immediate issues, list the consequences in the following categories:

❑ Desirable

❑ Possible

❑ Probable

❑ Inevitable

Desirable

This is what you want. But is it possible?

Delete the impossible. Don't ask for miracles.

* *Daydreaming does not help.*

Possible

If it is possible, then to what extent is it possible? What are the chances like? Are you worried about something that has only a one per cent possibility of happening? That way everything is possible! Earthquakes, floods, tsunamis, nuclear explosions, asteroids colliding with earth, etc., etc., , everything is possible. Can you afford to lose sleep over such things?

* *Do not be an inveterate pessimist.*

Probable

Are you sure it is very likely to happen? If yes, then this deserves serious consideration.

* *Consideration, not worry!*

Inevitable

This deserves immediate attention.

* *Attention, not panic!*

Do not jump to hasty conclusions. Think again. Review.

By doing this part of the exercise, you should zero down on the consequences that are most likely to happen in the near future.

Having listed all the possible consequences, rearrange them in order of gravity. What is the worst scenario? Will the consequence be your death? Or untimely death of a member of the family close to you? Will you have to go to prison? Are you going to lose all your money forever? Such grievous consequences have to be differentiated from such of the consequences that are likely to cause you discomfort, embarrassment, extra efforts or some loss of face.

If the consequences are vague and remote, forget about it. If the consequences are adverse and material in nature, and within the category of probable or inevitable, that too, in very near future, then go to step IV.

By such listing, you may yourself realise that the problem was not worth being worried about. With a little care and caution, you will be able to face the situation without much damage. In other words, you should by now be able to distinguish between being careless and being carefree, between being careful and being careworn. Only a careful person would be carefree. However, if the consequences are to be serious, it is time to act, and to act positively. For this, you need to find solutions, because unless your mind goes into the solution mode, stress would continue to be generated.

Step IV: Look for Solutions

Now that you have been able to understand the nature of the problem, have identified the cause and, after analysing all the facets, have some idea of the likely consequences, the time has come to find solutions. What you have to do is:

- ❑ Plan for the possible and desirable;
- ❑ Prepare for the inevitable and probable.

It is better to think about the solutions than to worry about the consequences. Discussing the issue with friends would also help. You have to plan and prepare yourself for the consequences. Your thoughts in the planning process should involve the following steps:

- ❑ **Writing the options.** Planning means taking decisions on the options that are available to you. For this you must know the options. Do you have any choice of action in the given situation? What are the options? List them. What steps can be taken at various stages? Often, there are no soft options. What has to be done has to be done. If it cannot be cured, it has to be endured. So do not look for an escape. It is better to face the problem than to try to avoid it. Avoiding it may only worsen the problem!

  Which of the options would you select? That will depend on your capabilities and resources. Therefore, go to the step mentioned below.

- ❑ **Listing your strong and weak points.** The selection of options will depend on this. This self-analysis has to be done one day. While the optimist exaggerates his strengths, the pessimist emphasises his weaknesses. Be rational, unemotional, and fair in your self-evaluation. We all have our strengths and weaknesses. What's important is that we know them, and their limitations.

  You cannot make any plan of action without knowing yourself, about what you can do and what you cannot. A good friend would be of immense help. Encourage him to be frank. Once you realise your own strengths and weaknesses, you would know how and when to plan your future strategy. Make best use of your strengths. You may finally realise that you are not as helpless as you had imagined yourself to be.

- ❑ **Seeking help from others.** Can you tackle the situation alone? Do not be shy in taking help. Do not keep problems to yourself. Mobilise other resources. Do you know who can help you? Think of all the hundreds of people you know. They can be your resource, and your friendship and acquaintance with them may be your untapped strength. Communicate and discuss things with others. List the people who can help you. Search for contacts. Actively seek assistance. There is nothing wrong in it. It is your right to seek support from the society. Do not incur material damage out of your conceit or bashfulness in seeking such support. Vanity never pays.

- **Thinking and finalising your Action Plan early.** Think! Do not be hasty. Do not take decisions on the spur of the moment. Decisions taken on impulse lack rationality, and often go wrong. (Like resigning from the job because you cannot get along with the boss!) At the same time, do not wait for the problem to vanish by itself. Untreated minor problems fester into major problems. Prepare your own action plan in time.
- **Starting work on the plan.** Once a rough plan is ready, do not hesitate in taking the first step. We are often so overawed by the entire problem, and so unsure of our plans, that we are afraid to even take the first step towards the solution. Let not the magnitude of the problem so daunt you that you become diffident about taking the first step. Remember, the first step taken is half the work done.

Try to solve the problem one step at a time. You may not find the entire solution right in the beginning, because the future is always uncertain, and new situations keep unfolding all the time. Take the one best step that you can take today. As you move ahead in time, the road will start becoming more and more clear, and new solutions will come up. If you do not move, you may miss the opportunities that are lying in wait for you. So do not be afraid of taking the first step. The road may be long and the journey may be tiring. So what? No one ever died from hard work alone! It is often not the problem that kills, but the worry about it that is fatal.

Adopting this method for solving problems has two fundamental advantages. The first is that doing this exercise clarifies your own thoughts about your problems. It clears confusion from the mind, which are often due to emotions clouding your thinking. Such an exercise helps in evaluating the causes and consequences of a problem, in crystallising your vague notions and fears and, finally, in transforming the problem into a rational action plan. Working on this action plan may help you in actually solving the problem.

The second advantage is that even if (and even while) the problem is not solved, your attention is at least diverted from the problems to the solutions. There are genuine and material problems in this world that have no immediate or easy solutions. We have to work hard and long to solve such problems. It is during this period when we are worrying about our problems that we come under stress. Our thinking remains negative and stress acts within us in a negative way. This is a damaging period.

On the other hand, when we have an action plan, our thinking becomes positive and the stress also becomes positive. Even if the immediate problem we face is not solved, at least the damage done by negative stress is controlled and our attitude remains positive. It is necessary that even while we are working towards solving our problem, we benefit from such an exercise that shifts our focus from problems to solutions, and relieves us from stress.

Improve Your Luck Through Work and Friends

Ultimately, it is your own hard work and the friends that you have made in your life that will help you solve your problems. Albert Einstein said that success is one per cent inspiration and 99 per cent perspiration. If you work hard with proper thoughtful direction, and develop a fair circle of right-minded friends, you would be indirectly improving your own luck. These are matters of attitude. The inclination to work hard is a matter of attitude, not intelligence.

The habit of cultivating a circle of good friends is also a matter of attitude. Ultimately, success depends more on attitudes than on talent or intelligence. Talent and intelligence are potentials for success. It is attitude that turns this potential into success. And attitudes can be developed by constant self-appraisal and conscious efforts. The exercise suggested in this chapter helps you in your self-appraisal.

Following the lane of intellect, you can take decisions in life on the basis of rationality, without being too overwhelmed by emotions. Using your intellect, you can take conscious decisions to change your attitudes. Thereby, you can turn your brain from a worrying machine into a problem-solving instrument. Let your intellect be a real friend to you, not your own enemy.

■■

Stress Management

Lane III

The Emotions

The development of intellect was followed by the evolution of emotional feelings among living beings. One essential difference between humans and animals is that the emotional dimension among humans is much more pronounced. Whereas animals, particularly mammals, do display certain primitive emotions, they are never overwhelmed by these. Animal emotions are simple and directly related to the survival instinct of the body. Animals love their owners, who feed them and impart a sense of security. But no animal would have compassion for someone not known to it.

Among humans, the emotional aspect is much more complex and often overwhelming. Human emotions are the making of the mind, and have a tremendous element of creativity of the human intellect. Often, the emotional facet predominates both the physical and intellectual aspects.

The emotional development of a human being depends on a combination and interplay of a large number of genetic and environmental factors. The body and the mind have direct and two-way relationships with the emotional aspect of man. The intellect and the body on the one hand help in developing the emotional build-up of man. The emotional set up, in turn, has a strong bearing on the body and the mind.

How Emotional Disturbance Creates Stress

Human beings are said to be social animals. We live in societies that have a social structure, a hierarchy, and certain norms that are observed by everyone. A family is the smallest unit of a society. It also has an unwritten code of behaviour and responsibility for each member. As we grow up, we imbibe these unwritten laws of family and social behaviour. We not only try to abide by the norms of the society but also develop similar expectations from other individuals, as well as from the society as a whole. This is to say that we inherit not only a conditioned body but also a preconditioned mind. Over the millions of years of development of man, we have been conditioned to accept and to expect certain norms of human behaviour. These are the paradigms of the mind.

An emotional disturbance takes place due to breach of paradigm of the mind. We start expecting certain rigid responses to be followed by everyone. When this does not happen, the paradigm is broken and we wonder what has happened. Our intellect is not able to resolve the conflict between what *is* and what *should have been*.

To cite an example, if you are working at a senior position in an organisation, you get accustomed to a certain type of behaviour from your subordinates, which is a mix of courtesy, respect and servility. You expect your driver and your peon to salute you every morning, and you just acknowledge the same in return by a gesture of a mere nod. If suddenly one day, these subordinates stop doing that, you will find it very strange and insulting. You will feel hurt, although they have not even touched you. In fact they have done nothing, they have not even wished you a good morning. All that they have done is that they have not done what you expected out of a long period of conditioning. Since you are not able to understand this change in behaviour, the paradigm is broken.

This is a life-threatening situation for the survival instinct, and cause for generation of stress. Adrenaline is rushed to physically meet with a situation that is not physical in nature at all. It is just an emotional problem, a conceptual problem, but the body knows only one way to counter all situations of stress. The rush of adrenaline leads to aggravation of emotional disturbance and affects the body as well.

When we are under stress, it is the emotional aspect that gets most disturbed or disoriented. The disorientation of this emotional make up, in turn, affects the brain. Not only does this disturb the normal functioning of the intellect (affects the rational thinking system of the intellect), but also adversely affects us physically in the sense that it disturbs the functioning of the regulatory mechanism of the endocrine system (the system of hormones). The brain controls and regulates the working of various systems in our body and maintains coordination and balance between different systems. Mental disturbances affect this. A perturbed mind loses the capacity of sustaining this balance between various systems. Over a period of time, some systems suffer due to hyperactivity, while certain other systems suffer due to inactivity.

To illustrate, let us look at our digestive system. The activities of the digestive system work on a need basis. From time to time, when the sugar level of the body is depleted, the body sends a signal to the brain about its requirement for food. This leads to a conscious decision by the mind to take food. When we eat food, an involuntary decision is taken by the brain to release gastric juices, which are essential for digestion. All future activities involved in the process of digestion are involuntary activities triggered by the brain. When we are emotionally disturbed, we may ignore the signals being given by the body for the intake of food. How often people forget to eat their meals in time when they are engrossed in some activity.

Even after eating food, the emotional disturbance may affect the involuntary activities controlled by the brain for food processing. This may lead to disruptions in the digestive system. People under stress frequently develop loss of appetite and other digestive problems.

Similarly, other body systems are also adversely affected during stress. Thus, any type of emotional disturbance leads to a disruption in the normal activity of the brain's regulatory system. Due to loss of balance between the various systems, the whole body is adversely affected. In the long term, it severely affects the immune system (power of resistance) in the body.

Hence, it is very necessary that you retain your emotional equilibrium. You have to make yourself emotionally strong so that you remain inured to external disturbances and do not get emotionally disturbed. If you were emotionally strong, your survival instinct would not take minor and petty breaches of paradigm as life-threatening situations. You have to get rid of fear and the sense of insecurity, which leads to an inferiority complex.

In order to achieve this you have to:

Increase your self-esteem.

We all carry a mental image of ourselves, and continuously evaluate ourselves according to that image. We feel nice and strong if that image looks good. The good image in our own eyes gives us a sense of self-respect. That is what we call self-esteem. Since this image depends upon our own activities and achievements, the better our achievements, the higher would be our self-esteem. When we fail to come up to our own expectations, it is this self-esteem that gets the biggest shock. We then consider ourselves inadequate and a failure.

This sort of feeling provokes the survival instinct to generate stress, because the survival instinct classifies every signal in only two categories: those conducive to survival and those that are a threat to survival.

Thus, even a minor failure can be classified as a threat to survival. Till we are not able to come out of this situation, the negative stress keeps working. Our inherent paradigm demands that either we solve the problem or we escape from the threats. A resolution, one way or the other, is required. Till we do not resolve the conflict and confusion, we would be under stress.

In today's world, we can neither solve all our problems, nor escape from them. We have to live with them, without being under stress. A higher level of self-esteem would make us feel more secure and let us live with the problems without treating them as life-threatening situations. For this, it is necessary that we raise the level of our self-esteem. But since we assess ourselves purely on the basis of our material achievements, and in comparison to other persons, we find it difficult to raise our self-esteem unless we have improved in our material achievements. It may not always be feasible for all of us to have significant material achievements to our credit. Hence we must analyse how to increase our self-esteem within our limited capabilities.

Self-esteem does not depend only on material achievements. It all depends on how we evaluate ourselves. Most of us neither have the potential nor the opportunities to win battles in war, receive a Nobel Prize, or bag a medal in the Olympics. That does not mean that we should lack self-esteem. Minor emotional achievements can also build up a good image. Even if we are not in a position to achieve major things, minor things done in day-to-day activities or any good work done helps in improving the image that we carry about ourselves.

Nothing helps in improving this image as much as helping others. In fact, when we are helping others, we are simultaneously also helping ourselves in the process by improving our own image. This is the reason why people involved in selfless and charitable activities are emotionally stronger. They carry a far better image of themselves and have a higher level of self-esteem.

In fact, we all want to perform selfless and charitable activities, because it makes us happy. We look for a readily available platform to do such activities, but often do not have one. Whereas a very large number of such organisations exist which provide a platform as well as scope for engaging in such activities, it may not always be possible for many of us to join them.

However, that should not deter you. Truly speaking, no platform is required. Even very small acts of kindness, like helping a disabled person cross the road or just being nice and polite to everyone, hardly take any time and need no platform. Such opportunities are available all the while and should never be lost.

Once in a while, go to a government hospital and you will find scores of poor and illiterate people in need of help. You need not spend your money on them if you do not want to. Proper guidance itself would be a great help, as they do not know where to go. Help someone to fill a form, and you will realise that even the most well educated person cannot fill a form properly. Guide the other to the office from where the blood report is to be obtained. These are major problems for an outsider, particularly if he is illiterate. You can be a great help there without spending money and you need no platform for such acts. And you would feel so good about yourself after you have helped a few persons. We may not be able to do big things, but we can always do a large number of small acts of kindness everyday. Over a course of time, one by one, such acts help in strengthening you emotionally.

We can take conscious steps to retain our sense of self-esteem, and keep ourselves emotionally strong so that problems, when they do occur, do not affect our body and mind.

By taking some of the following measures, this can be achieved:

Find Diversions

- ❑ **Keep busy.** An idle mind is the Devil's workshop. The faculty of creativity in the human mind is also a problem sometimes. When we are under stress, we think of our problems very aggressively and all the time. We get so involved and preoccupied with our problems that we can think of nothing else! Being idle affords us extra time to think of the problems. In fact, we create more problems in our mind than can ever physically exist!

Do not brood and sulk at such times. Keep yourself physically and mentally busy. This helps to keep you away from negative creativity of the mind. Any type of activity helps, especially constructive work, one that occupies you both physically as well as mentally at the same time. Doing some household chores, participating in social activities, or reading helps.

- **Engage in social service.** Nothing improves our sense of self-esteem as much as doing something for others. Do something for others every day. By helping others, you actually help yourself the most in terms of increasing your own self-esteem. See the happiness of people dedicated in some form of social work; it seems as if a powerhouse charges them internally.

  But it is not necessary that one must join a charitable organisation or some other institution for doing such work. Do join if you can. If you cannot, due to lack of time or otherwise, doing very minor things in everyday life also adds to your self-esteem. Helping children, the aged and disabled people at railway stations, bus stations, on roads etc. takes very little time and gives a tremendous sense of self-satisfaction.

Change Your Environment

If you are under severe stress, you may need to take more positive steps to change your environment. Here are some tips:

- **Pursue a hobby.** Do you pursue anything other than the work you do in your profession? You may have had hobbies, like painting, photography, writing a diary and the like, when you were young. You may have given these up over the years, partly because you thought you were not very good at it, and since you felt this hobby was not going to pay enough to be your profession. Later, you got busy with other activities of life and your profession.

This is everyone's life story. Resume the hobby that you gave up 30 years ago. If you never had a hobby, it is never too late to develop one. Try to take interest in new things. They would make your life more interesting. Try bird watching. It is very interesting and needs no expenditure. Even if you are not good at such extra-curricular activities, do not consider them a waste of time. In fact, these are investments to make you emotionally more stable, as they provide you a backup for relaxation.

- **Take a break.** Do you feel you have got into a rut and the daily routine of your job is getting you down? Step out of the normal routine once in a while. It is very helpful. Sometimes, in stressful situations, the daily routine (which contains the elements of stress) starts reinforcing the negative stress, and thereby accelerates the vicious circle. Occasional breaks from routine help in breaking the vicious circle.

  It is not necessary that you plan a long trip to some faraway place. Such a trip may be difficult to plan and would also be costly. Taking small holidays and simply going out to make a complete change from the daily routine for a day or two helps. Even a daylong picnic on Sunday with the family is better than sitting at home, watching TV and brooding about Monday.

- **Turn to nature.** When did you last *notice* a butterfly or a flower? Life is becoming too artificial these days. We live in synthetic houses, work in synthetic offices, walk on synthetic roads, move in cars and entertain ourselves through synthetic mediums. This is not good. We cannot live cut-off from nature without suffering emotional consequences.

  Nature is one of the best medicines for restoring the emotional balance in us. Is it not strange that although there are so many natural activities taking place around us all the time, we tend to overlook them? We are so preoccupied with our own problems and ourselves that we totally ignore what is happening in nature. Sunrise, sunset, the swirling of trees, blooming of plants in different seasons, the activities of birds and animals, all these occur around us all the time. It does not cost anything, not even time, to just watch them.

Going out for a brief walk in the garden and making conscious efforts to observe the behaviour of nature can greatly help in relieving ourselves from tension and in retaining our emotional balance.

- ❑ **Music can work wonders.** If you can play a musical instrument, or sing, it would be good to spend a little more time in this. However, listening to music in itself is quite rewarding. Every type of music is a good diversion. However, loud or melancholic music is likely to excite one or create sadness. This would increase stress. Sad music leads to self-pity, which can be dangerous. The best is Indian classical music, as it is spiritually uplifting. Devotional music based on Indian classical ragas is the best to ease all forms of tension. Many such cassettes and CDs are available in the market today.

- ❑ **Control your anger.** When things do not go the way we want them to, we feel threatened. Anger is one of the reactions by which the survival instinct tries to protect us from unfavourable situations. When we are angry, we are in a highly disturbed emotional state, because at that time there is a very strong rush of adrenaline.

  Emotions during anger so overwhelm us that we are in no position to apply the intellect. That is to say, we are not in a position to take rational decisions because anger clouds the intellect. In this state, when we are fully charged with adrenaline, we have no direction to put that into any constructive activity. It is this lack of direction that makes stress in such a state negative in nature and, thereby, only damages our system.

It has been well said in the *Bhagavad Gita* that anger robs us of discretion and, therefore, leads to destruction. That is why we are so often told that we must know how to control our anger. However, when I say, "control our anger", I do not mean that we should suppress it. Suppressed anger leads to impotent rage, which is as damaging as the anger itself.

There is another theory, which says that instead of suppressing anger we must vent it out somehow, like letting out steam through a safety valve. However, letting your anger out, in any way, also does not help. The state of anger leads to a high state of negative stress. What is necessary is to develop an attitude that ensures anger does not overwhelm you at all. This will depend on your outlook.

We will deal with the subject more specifically in the next chapter on spirituality.

- **Communicate!** Problems related to relationships can cause severe stress and may even lead to depression. People on strained terms with their colleagues, bosses, spouse or children are under constant stress. This is so because we have expectations from these people. The higher the expectation level, the more strained the relationship.

  However, most problems of relationships are fundamentally communication problems. When our feelings are hurt, we close our doors and go into a shell. This is a state of deadlock and stalemate. We hesitate in telling others about our feelings, and also do not encourage others to express their feelings. Ego also comes in the way.

  Therefore, we live in closed compartments, and keep expecting the other party to initiate steps to restore the relationship. However, this is a state of negative stress because there is no action plan for the solution. Such an impasse would not lead to any solution.

It is imperative that communication is immediately restored. Take the initiative. Open out and tell the other person all that you feel, all that hurt you, and certainly that you want to restore the relationship as normal. Do not attempt to win the argument in your favour. Only explain your feelings. And listen to the other person. It will make you feel good that you have risen above petty ego restrictions and taken the lead. The more you communicate, the better you would feel, and the better would be the chances of the problem resolving itself.

- **Everyone is different.** Variation is the way of nature. No two persons are exactly alike. And no two situations are exactly the same. As such, to expect everyone to behave in the same way is expecting the impossible. But since we are conditioned by our emotional paradigms, we often expect a set behaviour from other people. When this does not happen, we become tense and unhappy.

  We have to accept that different people will always react differently. In fact, even the same person would react differently under similar circumstances at different times, depending on his state of mind at each moment. As such, treat each individual and each situation differently.

  Provide space for differences even in most intimate relationships. Do not try to bind the other person entirely to you liking. No one is your slave. If you maintain such flexibility, and allow others to be different, you will have much better relationships.

- **Do not personalise issues!** One who does not respond according to your expectations is not your enemy. If someone does not agree with your views on a subject, you need not necessarily treat him as your opponent at a personal level. And do not think he would always be an antagonist. Do not take everything to your heart. Do not keep all the issues open all the time. Treat each event separately. Learn to close chapters after the issue is over. Learn to begin afresh.

Do not interlink events with people and make things personal. Treat people as people and events as events. These are different things. Do not mix up the two. The less you interlink, the less complicated would be your life. Try to keep things simple.

- **Don't be judgemental about people.** That someone has not been of help to you in one situation does not imply that he is an unhelpful person. Just as your failure in a venture does not mean that you are a dud for life. One cannot generalise. You can pass judgements over events, not on the people involved. Remember, everyone is different in different situations. Situations can be good or bad, actions can be good or bad, but try to keep relationships out of such categorisations. No one likes to be permanently categorised.

  Passing judgements over people only deprives you of plenty of potential supporters.

- **Start each day afresh.** Every day is a new day. What happened to you yesterday may not happen the next day. Memories of the past are helpful only to the extent that they help you plan your today and tomorrow better. Do not permit events of the past to cast a gloomy shadow over events that are yet to take place.

  Have the courage to make a fresh beginning. Do not prejudge your fate. Only plan for it.

- **Rationalise!** The human mind has infinite capacity to justify and rationalise things. It also has the same infinite capacity to confuse and complicate matters!

  It all depends on how you want to think. Positive thinking makes you see the brighter side, negative thinking leads to gloomy thoughts. Intellectual thinking is one where you see all the aspects and then take conscious decisions whereby you not only try to solve your problems, but also remain free from stress.

Try to evaluate situations with intellect, not with emotions. Rationalise in a positive way, to suit yourself. Do not unnecessarily make yourself unhappy.

- **Seek social support.** Many of us have great hesitation in seeking social support. We feel shy in telling others that we have a problem and need help. We feel guilty in doing so, as if we are taking an obligation. To some extent, this is also due to the survival instinct. We feel that if we openly express our problems we will be vulnerable and exposed to all sorts of threats. Therefore, we try to keep our problems to ourselves, often till it is too late.

We must remember that we are social beings. While on the one hand it is our duty to contribute our lot to society, it is also necessary that we understand that when we are in some problem we have the right to seek support from society. There is nothing wrong in seeking social support when we have a problem.

The key elements of seeking social support are:

- Do not suffer alone.
- Socialise, have friends, share your thoughts.
- Do talk to others about how you feel.
- You may realise that you are not the only one with problems.
- Problems have solutions that you are not aware of.

However, you must be very clear that you are seeking moral, material and/or social support, but not sympathy. Support and sympathy are two very different things. Support means help, sympathy means pity. Be careful about this.

> *Look for supporters and helpers, not sympathisers.*
> *Sympathisers only reinforce self-pity and lower self-esteem.*

Support means active and positive help, which will directly contribute in handling the problem that has caused you this situation of stress. It may be through material means or by intellectual means.

Sympathy, on the other hand, simply expresses regret for your situation. Words of sympathy always sound very good. Sympathy is a sort of courtesy, etiquette and good manners, meant more for exhibition and lip service rather than anything else. Sympathy superficially gives you a very good feeling. But actually it only reinforces your sadness, your sense of self-pity and your feeling of loss and failure. It erodes your self-confidence, makes you emotionally weaker and lowers your threshold level of threat percept of the survival instinct and thereby makes you more prone to stress.

Therefore, you should:

Never indulge in self-pity.

While sympathisers appear like nice, cultured and well-meaning people, in actual fact they unknowingly, unintentionally and indirectly reinforce your sense of self-pity and thereby do a lot of damage to your emotional resilience. Avoid them. Self-pity leads to persecution complex wherein the person thinks that everyone is against him and that everyone is plotting to make him unhappy. Fortunately, people are too busy to be so much concerned about you.

The question remains: *How and where do you get supporters from?*

By investing your time in the goodwill pool! If you have been helping others – without any motive of receiving anything in return – over a long period of time, you will find supporters automatically. Being good to others enhances your self-esteem and thereby makes you emotionally stronger. On the other hand, it has practical and material advantages in the sense that, over a period of time, you develop a circle of people who would come forward to help you when you need them.

However, good work should not be done with an eye on such material returns, but should rather be pursued as an end in itself. Let your investment in the goodwill pool give you returns without asking for it.

The Power of Autosuggestion

Think positive. We become what we think. We can strengthen ourselves emotionally by seeking support from outside factors, as mentioned earlier, and also by seeking support from our own self. This is known as *therapy through autosuggestion*.

Autosuggestion means consciously giving yourself positive messages that boost your self-confidence and make you emotionally strong. This would be particularly helpful in a situation where external social support is not available. Or if you may not like to share your problems with someone else, for whatever reason. Even if emotional support from outside is available, it is still very important that you also strengthen yourself internally, because you should always rely more on your own strength than on any external factor.

Autosuggestion does not mean self-denial or self-delusion. Lying to yourself will not help. Escapism never works. Autosuggestion means telling yourself that you have done your best and will continue to do so. Through this self-interaction, you can be in a position to increase your self-esteem.

Tell yourself:

- I can do this.
- I have done my part of the duty.
- This is what I have achieved.

> *You are not defeated till you accept defeat.*

We have briefly discussed the concept of training our mind earlier also. Therapy by autosuggestion depends on how you have trained your mind. You can psychologically train your mind to always adopt a positive and optimistic outlook. During the Second World War, when Great Britain was in a very difficult situation, the British Prime Minister Winston Churchill realised the significance of boosting the morale of his countrymen. His speeches were a great act of mass autosuggestion for a nation almost on the brink of defeat.

I quote an excerpt from one of his speeches:

"You ask, what is our aim? I can answer with one word: Victory – victory at all costs, victory in spite of all terror, victory however long and hard the road may be; for without victory there is no survival.... We shall not flag nor fail. We shall go on to the end. We shall fight in France and on the seas and oceans; we shall fight with growing confidence and growing strength in the air. We shall defend our island whatever the cost may be; we shall fight on the beaches, on landing grounds, in fields, in streets and on the hills. We shall never surrender..."

That should be your spirit, to continue with the struggle, determined that you would never surrender. Once that determination is ingrained in your psyche, that you would never accept defeat, the threshold level of the survival instinct would rise. Your attitude would be positive and your approach optimistic. You should continuously keep strengthening yourself emotionally by giving similar messages to yourself.

Coin your positive slogans:

- ❑ *I will* always remain strong.
- ❑ *I will* always continue to fight.
- ❑ *I will* never accept defeat.
- ❑ *I will* never lose hope.
- ❑ *I will* never break down.
- ❑ *I will* never give up.

Repeat your slogans when you wake up in the morning and at night before retiring to sleep. Repeat them whenever you feel you have been let down and feel low in spirits. Repeat them when you feel defeated, dejected and lost. Repeat them as often as possible till you succeed in hypnotising yourself to such an extent that nothing external can beat you down.

By thus making yourself emotionally strong, you would raise the threshold level of your survival instinct and be less prone to attacks of stress.

Children are Also Prone to Stress

We are often so preoccupied with ourselves that we forget that there are children at home. They are thinking beings with emotions similar to us. Do not think that stress is generated only among adults.

Children are as vulnerable to stress as adults; in fact, they may be even more vulnerable to stress! Children may not be able to express it, or they may not like to open out and tell you how they feel. Sometimes they are afraid to tell you, or want to avoid telling you things that they think might disturb you. They are not even very good at communication. It is for these reasons that children under stress become uncommunicative, and you may not be able to perceive that the child is under stress.

We must realise that children have their own world, quite unknown to elders. They have their own problems – at school, with teachers and friends and with studies. And because of competition and the high standards that we often inadvertently impose on them, they have great fear of failing and falling short of these expectations.

They listen with anxiety when adults/parents exchange hot words. They take these fights much more seriously than what the adults actually mean. They take the words at the face value, and get very worried about the consequences.

Children also have great fear of losing their loved ones, or of losing the love of their loved ones. Sometimes we ourselves threaten children with such possibilities, not realising that such threats linger in a child's mind for months, if not years. It makes him feel very insecure and vulnerable.

Since they are only children, they do not have any experience or skill to cope with stress. They have no strategy, and nothing to fall back upon. Such situations lead to a state of suppressed stress for which there is no outlet. Such emotional disturbance in children can greatly affect not only their development in childhood, but may also carry scars later in their life. For this reason, it is necessary to gradually educate children also about strategies to cope with stress.

The behaviour of elders at home and their interpersonal relationships have a tremendous bearing on the emotional state of children. Homes that have fights and tensions become dungeons for children where they feel trapped. Take care this does not happen in your home.

Therefore, it is very necessary that you:

Maintain a healthy and happy atmosphere at home.

Home is where you not only live but also have maximum emotional exchanges. Your home should be like a fort, to protect you from all external emotional disturbances. If your domestic front is strong, you can face the rest of the world.

Always maintain an atmosphere of happiness and gaiety at home. It helps you as well as your children.

■■

Stress Management

Lane IV

Spirituality

We have already discussed how to manage stress in the physical, the intellectual and the emotional components of our personality. Now we will discuss the philosophical aspect, that is, how to manage stress spiritually. As said earlier, life was first a body, and the mind developed afterwards. Emotions followed the development of intellect and, finally, the spiritual or philosophical aspect of human beings developed.

It is this philosophical aspect that distinguishes man most clearly from lesser animals. Whereas some animals do display certain emotions, none has shown any evidence of a spiritual dimension. The human being is complete with these four dimensions or components of personality. Stress has also to be managed in all these four aspects, and in the same order as they developed in humans.

In the subsequent pages, we will focus on managing stress spiritually. The route indicator to this lane reads:

> *Turn to philosophy.*

What is Philosophy?

Action is a must to sustain life. We all act. But do we ever pause and think about what exactly is going on? About why we act the way we do? And what the end purpose of all these activities is?

All of us engage in day-to-day activities, often without thinking about what exactly is going on. We tend to live on a day-to-day basis, reacting to each event, without seriously thinking about what exactly is the overall scheme of things in this universe. Why are we here? What is our role in the overall scheme of things? What is life? What is this whole drama unfolding before our eyes? But we don't think about these things. We are simply carried away by the occurrence of events. We fail to visualise the complete picture of life. We do not understand why things take place in the way they do.

In order to understand the underlying cause of all actions that are taking place around us, we need to have a philosophical perspective.

Unless we have such a solid foundation, on which we can firmly stand and examine as to what is happening and why, we would be floating like particles in the air, overtaken by the events around us. We would feel as if we have no control over ourselves. We are likely to simply drift along, misled by the reactions of our body, by the analyses of our intellect and by our emotions. This is because our body, mind and emotions are fundamentally reactive in nature. Guided by the survival instinct, most of the time our body, mind and emotions are only responding to external stimulus. These actions and reactions are basically short term in nature. But we should not let an unending series of such short term and temporary events take control of our life.

We cannot go on reacting in bits and pieces indefinitely. We need to look at the larger picture, the whole picture. We need to know the cause, the instruments, the purpose and the outcome of action, and our own role in the process. This is called the holistic view of life. Philosophy means having a holistic view, having knowledge of the total picture. Philosophy entails establishment of a co-relation between the individual and the total picture.

It is the philosophy of life that gives us stability, and a basis to study the stimulus, so that we react not just on the spur of the moment but in a more holistic way, keeping the total picture in mind. The philosophical or spiritual way of thinking is nothing else but keeping such a total picture in mind, so that the individual fragments of the total picture do not delude us. Philosophy establishes a relationship between the individual and the context of action, and thereby reveals the underlying meaning of the action.

Thereby, philosophy gives us stability, aplomb and serenity. Spirituality is an attitude of looking at things, events, and our own position, with a long-term perspective within the total framework of the working of the system of the universe. Spirituality is the faculty to come out of one's own body and mind and see the whole picture of life objectively, like a witness, without any like or dislike, without attachment or prejudice, and without any preconceived notions.

How Does Spirituality Help?

We have seen how we are controlled by the paradigms of the body and the mind. Whereas the body, the intellect and the emotions are based on the mechanism of the survival instinct, it is spirituality, the unique faculty of mankind, which is above any fear of survival.

The spiritual man is one who has conquered fear, or rather understood the fear. The spiritual man understands and accepts the inevitable, and tries to find joy in the system over which he has little control. Thereby, he uplifts himself from the restricting influences of the body, the intellect and the emotions. In fact the yogi, the spiritual man, is beyond and cut off from these factors that are limited by the fear of survival. Thus, a truly spiritual man can never be affected by the ill effects of negative stress.

I have earlier said that without taking care of the body there is no way of being saved from the ill effects of stress. This was not said with any intention to belittle the role of spirituality. The spiritual path transcends all the other three paths, and can even make them redundant, if followed with consistency. However, taking care of the body is most important because it is very difficult for an ordinary man to be a true yogi. To be a yogi requires a long period of training of the body and the mind.

And it is even more difficult to remain a yogi, because it requires constant control over the intellect. But the intellect is very fickle in nature. There are too many allurements and distractions in this world. There are so many stories in our mythology about austere yogis being lured by mundane things and losing their path. Since trust, faith and outlook are basically intellectual decisions, it does not take a long time for a man to change his decisions and, thereby, his outlook and his faith. Whereas matters of the mind can change overnight, the strength gained by the body will last longer. However, if one can truly attain the state of a yogi, then nothing else is required.

That is why, it is better to keep the body fit and at the same time develop a spiritual way of looking at this world.

Insight into Indian Philosophy

There are several philosophies in this world, some of these religious, some not. I have nothing to say about philosophies that I have not studied. I will only discuss the Indian philosophy of *Vedanta* as propounded in the *Upanishads* and the *Bhagavad Gita*, as this has given me all the answers that I needed to free myself from all delusions, and has relieved the stress and strains of my own mind.

I would also like to point out here that this ancient Indian philosophy should not be looked upon as the philosophy of a particular religion, because this philosophy developed, and became a way of life in India, much before the concept of religion arose. Indian philosophy does not divide people on the grounds of religion. It unites all living beings, with the term *sambhava* being propounded much before anyone even thought of secularism. Since *sambhava* is the essence of the *Vedanta*, it is the most secular teaching available on earth. We will discuss *sambhava* in more detail later in this chapter.

It is not possible to discuss the philosophy of the *Vedanta* or the *Gita* in great detail here. For more detailed study, there are many books available in the market, which can be read. However, since I consider the philosophy of the *Vedanta* and the *Bhagavad Gita* as the ultimate in clearing all human doubts and delusions, I will briefly discuss a few key concepts of this philosophy.

Brahman

According to the *Rig Veda*, the entire universe was initially concealed in a condensed state, which had no form or shape. That was Brahman, the imperishable one, in a dormant state. (Brahman should not be confused with the God Brahma, of the Brahma-Vishnu-Mahesh trinity). This primeval state of Brahman was neither matter nor non-matter, neither existent nor non-existent, neither being nor non-being, rather a sort of form of energy. Brahman has always existed. From this Brahman, and by its own volition/ desire (out of its own internal energy/dynamics) the entire existence that we see came into being.

Another interpretation can be that the entire existence always existed because Brahman is the existence. All that happened was that Brahman unveiled the existence, and so it is now apparent to our organs of senses.

Brahman is not a god in the traditional sense. One should not confuse it with a living god. The main characteristics of Brahman as described in *Vedanta* are:

- Brahman is not a god. It is neither a thing nor a person.
- Brahman is not conscious in the way we understand a conscious being.
- Brahman does not take decisions on human affairs.
- Brahman is neither living nor non-living, or is both.
- Brahman is *nirguna* – it does not have any material qualities. It has no form. It is material as well as non-material.

Maya and *Prakriti*

Brahman is not something away from or superior to living beings. We all are part of a common source of the eternal cause, which is Brahman. All that we see, living or non-living, is a manifestation of one Brahman.

But we see infinite variations in this world! This is *Maya,* the power of creation. It is because of *Maya* that we see different types of living and non-living things, created out of the same fundamental source, that is, Brahman. It is *Maya* that creates all these variations through the force of Nature (*prakriti*). It is this *prakriti* that acts upon different things and causes them to become different and to behave differently (gives different properties to different things). Or rather, it is *prakriti* that makes certain inherent traits or properties (*gunas*) innate in various existences to become active and predominant.

All living and non-living beings, though formed from the same Brahman, are under the control of *Maya,* and are guided by their natures. *Maya* binds living beings to actions as well as to the fruits of their actions. To that extent, they have no independent identity or control over their own actions.

Sambhava

Chapter VI of the *Gita* deals with the concept of having *sambhava,* the attitude of equivalence or sameness in everything. *Sambhava* literally means having the same (equal) feeling towards everything. The man of knowledge realises that the entire universe is nothing but different forms or manifestations of the same Brahman. Everything is basically the same. It is only Nature (*prakriti*) acting upon matter that has made things different. Thus, there is nothing good or bad, nothing small or big, nothing attractive or loathsome.

Nature has not only made material things different, but also it is Nature that is making people act in the way they do. In fact, men are like puppets in the hands of their nature (helpless instruments in the hands of the great cosmic force of *Maya*). Therefore, the differences that we see are only superficial, created by Nature. Otherwise, everything is the same.

This is why the yogi has the same feelings towards everyone and everything. He sees Brahman in everyone and in everything, and thus does not discriminate between the two. The yogi realises that everything and every being is nothing else but Brahman only. He himself is also Brahman. As such there is no reason to assume any difference between individuals. The yogi sees everything in oneness with himself. Therefore, there is no reason for ego and he is neither attached to anyone nor does he abhor anyone, because everyone is the same to him.

Each of us, however, sees a situation individually and, therefore, differently. We see things according to our own mindset, with our preconceived notions, through the filter of our extant value systems and in relation to our own context. Hence, there can be no absolute evaluation of a situation or a problem. It can only be relative, in terms of the individual and his situation. Thus, everything is contextual.

Where we see a situation as a problem, others who are out of the situation see no problem at all. The true yogi, the man of knowledge, knows that whereas everything has the same source or origin, that is, Brahman, everyone sees the same thing differently because of each one's nature acting differently on different people at different times.

Since the yogi realises that it is only the force of *Maya* that is causing actions to take place, and all material things (living as well as non-living) are only instruments, he is neither sad nor excited or angry about any action that is taking place.

Therefore, realising all actions as the movement of the wheel of Brahman, the yogi is always at peace with himself. And, thereby, he maintains *sambhava,* i.e. equilibrium, in all situations. He retains his poise and is not swayed by anything.

Nishkama Karma

The above term means doing work without the feeling of being the doer. Everyone has to perform actions to sustain life. Even the yogi has to act. But when action is done with the expectation of achieving results, man gets attached to the results. This attachment leads to grief. Since results depend upon a very large number of other factors, man cannot control the results, and attachment to results only leads to worry and unhappiness.

This attachment arises due to ignorance about the cosmic system of god, the *Maya*. If man thinks that he can control the results, he comes to grief. If one acts without being attached to the results, he would never come to grief. However, the yogi realises that even while he is performing actions, actually it is Nature that is using his physical and mental faculties as instruments to get an action done.

As Krishna says, God pervades the individual Self and since God is not attached/imbued with His own actions, there is no reason for the individual to be so attached (XIII–31, 32). Thus, the yogi feels he is not the doer of the actions he himself is doing. Therefore, he has no attachment to the results of his actions.

Such work done with detachment is called *nishkama karma*. This freedom from attachment is liberation.

Moksha

In the *Isha-Upanishad* it has been said that nothing belongs to the individual; therefore, there is no need for attachment or ego. One who is not attached to anything is the one who is truly liberated. In the *Upanishads,* freedom from ego has been called *Moksha,* the ultimate liberation. *Moksha* is not just freedom from the cycle of rebirths, as is often misunderstood. It is simply the freedom from mental bonds on earth itself. It is the freedom from the bondage of works. It is not freedom from work but from its attachments. It is the freedom from the worries of the consequences of the actions. This is to be achieved through the practice of Yoga and self-realisation.

Moksha or salvation is also termed *mukti* or freedom. It is not something one achieves after death only. It has to be attained in this world. *Mukti* is not freedom from action (because man has to act all the time in order to live). *Mukti* is freedom from the bondage of works. This bondage is due to attachment towards one's self, hence towards the results of one's own actions.

Three Paths to Salvation

There are different types of people in this world, with different natures. Everyone cannot follow the same path. It is not even necessary that everyone follow just one path to achieve freedom.

In the *Bhagavad Gita,* Sri Krishna says that there are three ways of obtaining freedom or *mukti* from bondage. Man should understand his own nature and follow the path most suited to his nature. The three paths are:

a. ***Bhakti Yoga.*** This is the path of devotion. In this path, the devotee gives up his entire sense of ego and puts his absolute and complete trust in God. He unconditionally surrenders himself to the care of God, accepts whatever is happening as an act of God and thereby relieves himself both from the sense of responsibility as well as from the sense of guilt for whatever is taking place.

   In *Bhakti Yoga,* nothing other than complete devotion is required. Neither reading of Scriptures nor the following of any ritual is needed. It is the easiest of the three to practise for an ordinary man, and it never fails to deliver the devotee from bondage.

b. ***Gyan Yoga.*** This is the path of knowledge. In this method, man comes to understand Brahman, which is the system of this universe, through knowledge and practice (*sadhana*). Through this knowledge he understands how the system of the universe is operating. He also understands his own role in this cosmic system and his own significance (or insignificance) in the system. He understands that it is Nature that is operating on material existences and making actions take place over which he has no control. He can act but cannot control the results, as they depend on uncontrollable factors.

Once he understands the working of this *Maya*, he becomes detached and thereby attains peace of mind. He becomes a yogi, a man of wisdom. This path is for those few who can attain this level of knowledge.

c. ***Karma Yoga.*** This is the path of action. Here, man completely and sincerely devotes himself to do the duties assigned to him. He accepts that the cosmic system has assigned a role for him, and he has to perform that role and discharge responsibilities entailed with that role. (Since Arjuna is from a warrior class, and since his family has to fight a battle with the Kauravas, it is incumbent upon Arjuna to fight, because that is the role assigned to him). He does work because he realises that it is incumbent upon him to do so. He finds satisfaction and peace of mind in doing his work, without being attached to the results. He finds happiness in excelling in his work. This method is for those who are busy and engaged in their day-to-day activities. Those people who remain committed and devoted towards their work, irrespective of the results, attain peace of mind through the work.

Thus, for different types of people, depending upon their own nature, there are different ways of attaining *mukti*. It is important that the individual understands his own nature and then follows one of these paths in order to attain peace of mind, even as he is engaged in doing everyday mundane works.

The Essence of Philosophy

Having briefly discussed some of the key concepts of Indian philosophy, we can now take the essence of some of these in our practical day-to-day life. Certain important things that we learn from this philosophy are:

- **Everything is temporary.** In the *Mahabharata*, when the *Yaksha* asked Yudhishthira what the greatest wonder in the world was, Yudhishthira replied that everyone knows the fact that one has to die, yet everyone acts as if he is immortal. This was the greatest wonder.

  Similarly, even today, we behave and act as if we are here for good. We tend to overestimate our problems, as if these problems are permanent. We forget the fact that when life itself is temporary, nothing can be permanent. We rarely view our problems in the backdrop of the transitory nature of everything. We must always keep this in mind that neither our problems nor our physical body happen to be immortal. Everything is temporary and continuously changing.

  So, should we trouble ourselves unduly for things that are of a short duration only?

- **Life is a short journey on earth.** What is life? It is a short span of time that the body has to spend on earth. This time can be spent in happiness or in unhappiness. Whereas some suffering and unhappiness would come to us from the situations of this world, we can at least decide that we would not ourselves do anything that may make us unhappy, that there is no point spoiling this brief time by our own thinking and our own acts.

- **Nothing is really very important.** We feel that we are important enough for the situation to change itself to suit our requirements. We also feel that situations are important enough to feel happy or sad about. But situations keep changing. Everything keeps changing. This is a dynamic world and nothing is permanent.

  If everything is temporary, then nothing is really very important. Then why worry too much?

- **Everything is not in your hands.** Everything is not because of you. Many of our problems arise because we attach too much importance to ourselves. We think that we are in charge of things and that everything depends on us. We get worried and anxious when we find that while we should be in charge of the situation, this is not actually so.

We are psychologically not ready to accept this state of our inadequacy and insignificance in the scheme of things. We feel we can change the situation, or should be able to change it, but are annoyed at our inability to do so. It hurts our ego.

Since the whole world cannot act in concert for our satisfaction, we are likely to remain anxious and unsatisfied most of the time. In our effort to control everything, we often fail. Then we feel guilty about our own failures. We have to free ourselves from the delusion that we are in charge of situations.

Get rid of guilt. You are not god.

You must remember that some of the disadvantages of not being a god are that you would often fail, you would not get everything you want, you would suffer pains and ailments and there would be many needles to prick your ego.

Be prepared to face all this. But if you are able to think of yourself as a non-doer, like a yogi, then you rise above the concepts of failure and guilt, because you feel you are not doing anything and, therefore, you cannot fail.

Then there is no room for regret, disappointment or unhappiness.

What is Fate?

When the *Gita* talks about detachment from results of the action, does it mean that man should leave things to his luck? Should he become fatalistic? Should he just resign himself to his fate?

No!

When one is depending on luck, he is still not detached. A fatalistic man is only trying to depend on luck to achieve the results he desires, to which he is attached. Only, he is not depending on his own actions. Thus, he is not performing his duties, and such an attitude does not lead to liberation. Liberation has to be from the results, not from the actions. There is no room for inaction in the philosophy of the *Gita*.

We often fail to distinguish between detachment and inaction, and tend to look towards luck to bring us favourable results. When we fail, we have a tendency to blame our luck for our misfortunes and our state of unhappiness. This is especially so when we are in a state of stress.

We feel that we have been specifically earmarked for the misfortune that has befallen us, although we have not done anything to deserve it. This generates self-pity. We have already discussed that thinking along the negative lines of self-pity only lowers our resolve to remain strong in the face of adversity. Such negative thinking weakens us emotionally by lowering our self-esteem. As mentioned earlier, while we must take steps to keep our morale high, it is also necessary to examine what is meant by fate.

In the *Bhagavad Gita*, Krishna says that He does not pass judgements upon the acts of human beings. Even otherwise, to think that God keeps awarding and punishing people for their various acts is taking too petty a view of God.

To quote select *shlokas* from the *Gita*:

न कर्तृत्वं न कर्माणि लोकस्य सृजति प्रभुः ।
न कर्मफलसंयोगं स्वभावस्तु प्रवर्तते ॥

Na kartritvam na karmani lokasya srijati Prabhuh
Na karmaphalasanyogam svabhavastu pravartate

God creates neither the acts, nor the cause, nor the circumstances of the actions (or their fruits). It is Nature that acts these out (takes its course of action). (V, 14)

नादत्ते कस्यचित्पापं न चैव सुकृतं विभुः।
अज्ञानेनावृतं ज्ञानं तेन मुह्यन्ति जन्तवः ॥

Nadatte kasyachitpapam na chaiva sukritam vibhuh
Agyanenavritam gyanam tena muhyanti jantavah

God regards neither sin nor piousness of men.
It is ignorance that ensnares everyone. (V, 15)

न च मां तानि कर्माणि निबध्नन्ति धनञ्जय।
उदासीनवदासीनमसक्तं तेषु कर्मसु ॥

Na cha mam tani karmani nibadhnanti dhananjaya
Udasinavadasinamasaktam teshu karmasu

These actions do not bind Me as I stay
Unaffected and unattached to these works. (IX, 9)

Do not treat misfortunes as punishments.
This is a very negative view of life.
Treat misfortunes as accidents of life.
And do not blame yourself for them.

Understanding how this world works is one of the biggest mysteries for all of us. Despite scientists working hard to understand various aspects about the working of this universe, even today we can hardly explain anything in complete perspective.

The knowledge that we have today is in bits and pieces. Even this knowledge is also about how things work. There is no understanding about why things work the way they do. Despite such ignorance about the workings of the system of *Maya*, we like to think that everything works according to a laid-down system, and that we should be in a position to understand it. However, as Sri Krishna says in the *Gita*, the system of His *Maya* is mysterious and it is not possible for man to understand it.

To quote the *Gita*:

दैवी ह्येषा गुणमयी मम माया दुरत्यया।
मामेव ये प्रपद्यन्ते मायामेतां तरन्ति ते॥

Daivi hyesha gunamayi mama maya duratyaya
Mameva ye prapadyante mayametam taranti te

This three-faceted Maya *(creation) of Mine is difficult to fathom but those who concentrate on Me find their way out of this* Maya. (VII, 14)

You can free yourself from the bondage of *Maya* (by adopting one of the three paths mentioned earlier) but you can neither understand it, nor can you control it.

Thus, on occasions when we feel that some denial of justice has been done to us by God, we must also realise that we do not know what exactly is happening, or why.

There may be things that we feel are unfair or unjust, according to our way of thinking. But do we know how this entire system works? And can we control it as per our wishes?

No!

We must realise that we are like twigs flowing in a current of time over which we do not have any control, whether we like it or not. In this all-powerful torrent some of the twigs would be washed towards the banks, some could crash with boulders and some would keep drifting. The torrent would even slash the banks and smash the boulders into each other. That is how the life is. It is a difficult thing to accept, but acceptance of this fact alone can bring us peace of mind.

Accept that things are not perfect in this world and Nature does not know the meaning of justice.

The ticket system. This is a way I often try to describe the journey of life. During this journey, like any other journey, rather a series of journeys, you have to change the transport many times. Sometimes the vehicle will be good and the road smooth, at other times the vehicle will be creaky and the road bumpy. But you have no choice.

For this journey you have been issued a ticket by destiny (or by God, as you may like to say). The ticket that you have been given entitles you (or does not entitle you) to certain perks and privileges. Like if you are travelling in the Executive or Club class in an airline you are getting certain extra privileges which are not there for the economy class passengers. Or what you get as an AC first-class passenger in a Rajdhani you do not get as a second-class passenger of a passenger train. You have to accept that you will get what your ticket entitles you to. There is no point grudging what you do not have.

In fact, there is no point evaluating the occurrence of events according to our parameters of justice and injustice. The laws, and the Constitution that we follow, are made by human beings and are meant for human beings. The law of Nature, or the law of *Maya*, has nothing to do with the laws made by men. *Maya* has its own system of operation, which we can neither comprehend nor control. We should take it in due stride, as it comes, without pronouncing judgement upon it from the human point of view.

Can We Influence Fate?

In a philosophical way – yes, we can influence our own fate.

In the *Ashtavakra Gita*, it is truly said: *"As you think, so is your fate."* Our destiny is often decided by the way we think and act. It is mostly in our mind, not anywhere outside. If we take such conscious decisions that would bring us health and happiness, our fate would be good. On the other hand, if we involve ourselves in petty things, if we do not care for the health of our body and mind, we would only be unhappy. But if we retain a positive attitude, carry on with our work in life, taking adversity in due stride and taking good care of our health, we would be comparatively happy.

Unforeseen accidents can happen to anyone. You cannot always avoid or control them. But you can react towards them differently. That is in your hands. It depends on your outlook, on your attitude towards what is happening to you, on your philosophy of life. It depends on whether you are being your own friend or your own enemy. That is your fate.

It is often very strange that we observe one person taking decisions inexorably leading to his own destruction. During the later stages of World War II, the German dictator Adolf Hitler was told repeatedly that he was leading his country to disaster. Still, he refused to even consider any sensible suggestion or undertake any positive action and ultimately led his country to ruin and his own inexorable death. Hitler's fate was decided nowhere else except in his own warped mind.

Ravana and Duryodhana are other such examples of men who sealed their own fate by their pride and arrogance.

It is hence necessary to review our thought system periodically – about how we think, what we think and whether the way we are looking at things is going to lead us to happiness or unhappiness.

Therefore, we have to ask ourselves the basic question whether we are acting like our own friend or our own enemy. An answer to this simple question will make us review and even change our attitude and thereby significantly help even in changing our fate.

Having a philosophical or spiritual bent of mind helps us view the activities of everyday life in a wider perspective. It is necessary that we try to rise above narrow thoughts attached to the self, and try to see things in totality. It would give us a proper perspective of the things we see, rather than what we perceive when we see everything through the eyes of our own survival instinct.

■■

The Secret of Happiness

Having discussed various aspects of stress and how to control it in the previous chapters, in this last chapter, we will now discuss the ultimate objective of human life – happiness.

Happiness as a concept is unique to human beings. Animals can have sensations of security, satisfaction, pleasure and enjoyment. But happiness is something over and above these sensations. Happiness is something sublime – a feeling that is higher than the sensations of security, satisfaction, pleasure and enjoyment.

Then how do we define happiness? Although it is very difficult to define, we can surely identify some of the key elements of what constitutes happiness.

- Happiness is not a momentary sensation. It is a long-term feeling.
- Happiness does not erode. It has an element of permanency or durability.
- Happiness is basically self-generated: it does not depend on outside factors.
- Happiness is associated with peace of mind. It brings tranquillity; at the same time, peace of mind is a prerequisite for happiness.
- Happiness spreads to others. It is never at anyone's cost.

Having identified the key components of happiness let us examine where our pursuit of happiness is leading us.

Throughout our lives, we keep aspiring for many material and emotional things, like money, power, status, physical pleasures and sensations etc. We apply all our intelligence and spend much of our time and energy in chasing these things. We pursue the acquisition of these things with such energy and enthusiasm that we forget these are not ends in itself. They are means to a greater thing, and that is happiness. However, our pursuit of the means to happiness often causes us all the unhappiness. This is so because we often do not know how to remain happy. Or rather, we often do not remain conscious of the end goal, that is, happiness.

Unless we consciously desire happiness, and nurture the things that would make us happy, we would only be engaged and lost in acquiring the means to happiness, while happiness itself would elude us. We have to cherish happiness as the main objective of life.

You should be conscious that your ultimate goal is happiness, not the means to happiness. Your prime motto should be to:

> *Cherish happiness.*

To many of us, happiness seems to be something elusive, something that is not with us right now, but might come sometime later in life, if we achieve a particular thing, or if we reach a particular situation. It seems like a mysterious thing that is likely to come to us sometime in the future, like a milestone that we would pass one day.

I have seen so many people passing their precious days of life in unhappiness, doing their daily chores grudgingly and saying that they would be happy only after they reach a certain stage of life or pass a certain goalpost. These may be:

- ❏ Once their children are settled.
- ❏ They get that final promotion.
- ❏ They retire (and get out of that lousy job).

Unfortunately, this never does happen. Once they cross one goalpost, they find another one standing before them. Solving one problem makes way for another one. That is how life is, always changing. Those who think that happiness might come sometime later in their life may never receive happiness.

That mysterious happy day when everything would be fine never comes. That is utopia. Such a time, or such a place, when/where everything is perfect does not exist anywhere. Such a time never comes. Even if it does come, how can you be sure it would not change the very next day. So why keep all your happiness pending for that elusive day?

Do not wait for or dream about that day. You should not postpone happiness to that unknown and indeterminable day.

Happiness is something you should try to attain right now, today itself. And it is possible. In fact, happiness is waiting for you, here. You must firmly believe that:

You can be happy today.

The question is how? I know you want to live a happy life. We all want to be happy. But how do you expect happiness to come to you, and from where? Therein lies the problem!

- You expect and want happiness to come to you from some outside source.
- You keep hunting and searching for that unknown source.
- And you keep waiting.

Remember, happiness does not come
from any outside source.
It can come only from within you!

In fact, the most important thing about happiness is that it does not come at all. It does not have to come because it is already within you. It springs from inside. You have to realise it, unfold it and kindle it, like a candle of light inside you. Once lit from within your soul, this light can never be extinguished.

The question is: have you taken a decision that you will try to always be happy? It is the most important decision to be taken. You have to consciously take this decision. Once that decision is taken, you have to consciously examine each of your thoughts and actions, as to whether they are contributing towards your happiness or unhappiness.

You have to ask yourself whether your thoughts and actions bring you peace of mind or cause you tension and worries. Such introspection would help you change your attitudes. Because happiness is basically a state of mind, attained by a framework of attitudes and outlook.

It is for you to decide how you will act and think, for happiness or otherwise. It is in your hands. Ultimately:

You have to decide that you will be happy.

Happiness is not something that someone or something gives you. Happiness is something you give to yourself. But what do we try to give ourselves? We strive for money, material possessions, social status and position, physical comforts and pleasure.

We search for happiness among such things to such an extreme extent that possessing these things becomes an end in itself. We chase these things, as if this is our one and only goal. In the process we incur stress, lose our peace of mind and attain only unhappiness. We forget that these things can at best be only a means to the ultimate end called happiness.

One is not saying that material possessions or social status are not important. They certainly are. The question is – to what extent are these important? I quote from the *Upanishads*:

ईशावास्यमिदं सर्वं यत्किञ्च जगत्यां जगत्।
तेन त्यक्तेन भुंजीथा मा गृधः कस्य स्विद् धनम् ॥

Ishavasyamidam sarvam yatkinch jagatyam jagat
Tain tyaktain bhunjitha ma gridah kasya svid dhanam

Whatever exists in the universe is pervaded with God. Keeping God with self, enjoy existence with abandonment and do not get attached. To whom can the worldly treasures belong?

In brief, it means that there is no harm in enjoying the possessions of existence till such time that you are not attached to them (dependent on them).

If you link your happiness with any worldly thing, because of the temporary nature of worldly things, you are likely to remain unhappy most of the time. And you would keep losing your peace of mind in the effort to gain them. So it is not worldly possessions that are bad, but attachment to them.

Further, one is also not saying that worldly possessions and happiness are mutually exclusive, and that you cannot have both at the same time. You can be rich, powerful and happy at the same time. It depends on how you maintain a balance between various things. If you feel money is more important than peace of mind, then so will it be. The question is only of priorities. In fact, life consists of a wide choice of priorities.

There is often a discussion about what is the right attitude? To be ambitious, to strive for a better life, or to be just satisfied with what you have. I do not think that the two are mutually exclusive. One should strive for betterment of the quality of life. There is absolutely nothing wrong in having a higher status, more money and comforts. Why not? Ambition is necessary for all development. After all Krishna also exhorts Arjuna to fight the battle so that he can enjoy the fruits of Kingdom. The main thing is that as part of one's philosophy of life one should not get so attached to such goals, and ambitions, that unless you achieve them you cannot remain happy. One should also remember that there is a ticket in your pocket that controls your journey.

You can remain possessive about material things and make yourself miserable, or you can have a detached outlook, and be free of mental strife. This is a matter of attitude or outlook. You cannot get everything in life. So you have to set your priorities, depending on your nature. But do think about yourself and then set your priorities. How you decide your priorities often decides your fate.

When you go to a shop to buy a shoe, you buy the one that fits you best, the one you are most comfortable to walk in. You do not buy a shoe just because it looks good in someone else's feet. Then why in this life you hanker for things that may not even fit you? Measure your feet and think of the road, then buy your shoe.

Everything depends on your own outlook.

We have to understand that there is no one true picture of this universe. Similarly, there is no single angle from which life can be viewed in totality. There are many ways of looking at a thing and there are several facets of every situation. However, because of our own internal fears we have a very limited vision. We do not develop the attitude of taking a holistic view of situations. We want to see everything from one angle only. This is because of that intense survival instinct in us that often restrains us from taking a complete picture.

Once on my way to deliver this lecture I was stranded in a traffic jam. I being very conscientious about being punctual suddenly became tense that I was going to be late. What will all those waiting for me think? I thought for a moment, in anxiety. Then it occurred to me why should I get tense. Let those waiting for me get tense. Let the organiser of the lecture be tense. Why should I be tense? This thought suddenly made me calm. In fact it made me laugh to think that this situation could also be viewed from another angle. Being in a traffic jam I had no control over the situation. I had no choice over the circumstances. I had to wait till the jam cleared. But whereas I had no choice, or control over the situation, I did have a control over how I was to look at it. If I got tense, then I was handling over the control over myself to a traffic jam. But viewing the same situation from a different angle I was retrieving the control back into my hands. Either way the physical situation was not going to change. But I could avoid the tension, and laugh about not only my own predicament but also of those who were waiting for me. This was an act of rationalising the situation and thereby consciously looking at the better side.

Always look towards happiness.
And NEVER towards unhappiness.

There are two ways of looking at anything: the positive way and the negative way. You can be happy about what you have or you can be unhappy about what you do not have.

This is a matter of attitude, or outlook, which you can change. Attitude classifies stimuli into negative and positive categories. You can consciously take decisions in one classification. It is for you to either consciously and rationally take such decisions, or let your natural emotions take such decisions for you. It is your fate to decide which way you wish to look at things.

One of my friend's sons met with a serious road accident and ended up with multiple fractures in a hospital. A truck had rammed into the car he was driving, and the car was also smashed. One of his aunts was lamenting at the hospital as to what ill stars the unlucky boy had been through (she was a sympathiser, not a supporter). I said this was a matter of extreme luck that the boy had survived such a ghastly accident. This was not the angle from which the aunt was willing to see.

You have to develop a mental mechanism to view every situation from different points of view. If you are able to see a thing from different angles, only then can you get a more realistic picture of a situation. It depends totally on you, as to which of these pictures you accept as a true picture. You should accept the picture that gives you peace of mind and not a picture that disturbs you.

If you look only at the negative side, you would remain unhappy. Do not permit your petty emotions to take control over you. If you decide to view things with a positive frame of mind, you can remain happy.

A happy man will always retain control over his happiness by consciously keeping a positive outlook. Thereby, he remains a master of his own happiness. It is imperative that you should:

Be a master of your own happiness.

We often do not remain conscious of this fact and let our emotions take charge and subvert our happiness. Even worse is the situation when we make other people a master of our own happiness.

Let us look at a situation in everyday life. You are doing a job, and you get paid for it. But you are not happy. You feel your job is boring, monotonous and tiresome. No one appreciates the hard work you are doing. You want appreciation, don't you? Why? Because you want happiness!

You have unwittingly and unknowingly made yourself a slave of some other person, without his asking or wanting to be a master of your own happiness.

Every year when the time comes for recommending annual awards in my organisation, I find certain individuals desperately trying to get their name recommended. They throw hints, and sometimes blatantly supplicate for the same. They remain tense for a couple of months till the list of awards is released. When they fail to get the same, they become even unhappier. I pity them. Without any reason, they not only place the control of their happiness in someone else's hands, they also unnecessarily create a situation in which they are bound to be unhappy. If they had continued with their work, without expecting such awards to make them happy, they would not have been unhappy.

How many times in our daily lives do we get offended when we find others not responding as we expect them to respond? We expect so much from others, from our bosses, colleagues, friends, spouse, children, and when we find them not doing what we would like them to do, we sulk and are unhappy.

A colleague organises a birthday party of his son and invites me. I do not go. He gets displeased. I wonder why? I have not done anything that could damage him. Yet he wanted control over me, and his failure to do so aroused a threat, causing stress and anger. All of this was not warranted.

Not only do we link our happiness to our own possessions, but we also want to control others. Worst of all, we want other living and thinking beings to act as we would like them to, and when this does not happen, we feel unhappy. Thus we link our happiness to the actions of others, not to our own actions and, thereby, we make ourselves a slave of others for our own happiness.

The key to happiness is:

> *Do not depend on others for your happiness.*

We often look for awards, appreciation and approval from other people to make us happy. Such occasions or gestures do make us happy, but these do not come everyday, and even when they occur, they last only for a very short time. If you depend on any external thing or person to give you happiness, you would never find happiness. Remember that each individual is a different person, living in a world of his own, over which you have no control. Every time everyone will not respond as you want. Be prepared for this, and do not depend on it for your happiness.

Similarly, if you depend on any material thing to make you happy, then you are again linking your happiness to an inanimate object, which is least concerned about you or your happiness. There are many pitfalls in such an endeavour. You may not get that object. Even if you get it, it may not last long. And even if it lasts long, you would get so used to it that it would progressively give you less and less pleasure, never happiness, and you would start your pursuit for another object. This is an endless race, which brings more misery than satisfaction and never brings happiness. In essence, it is wrong to depend on material objects for happiness.

Another mistake we often make is that we entertain a vague notion that the coming of happiness is like a turning point in life. We often think that achieving happiness is a major event of life, or that some major event can bring happiness, like winning a lottery. Major events occur very rarely, and if we keep waiting for such turning points to make us happy, then we would only be waiting for happiness most of the time.

Happiness is not a meteor that hits you once in a lifetime. If you wait for great moments of achievement to bring you happiness, such moments would come, if at all, after long gaps, and with lots of anxiety and unhappiness in between. Therefore, do not wait for milestones to bring you messages of happiness. Invoke happiness at every step that you take.

Furthermore, do not wait for happiness to come in one huge lump. Happiness is not a piece of rock that falls before your feet. The consignment of happiness is made up of very small fragments that you can accumulate in bits and pieces every day. Happiness is not something solid that you can touch, see or pick up on your way home. Happiness is like a breeze of fresh air, all around you, always with you. You have to breathe it into your system. So do not wait for big chunks of happiness.

Add up small bits of happiness everyday.

Many successful adults lament that they ignored their family life when they were younger and were busy in the rat race for success. They regret that they did not spend more time with their children when they were small. But now it is too late. They have achieved success, but at a very heavy cost. That time has gone past. They have lost track of their friends. They have forgotten their hobbies. Those beautiful years of their kids' childhood have been lost forever, as time cannot be reversed.

Why did this happen? Because they thought happiness was something that required a whole lifetime's effort to achieve, and they ignored the small bits of happiness that were available to them in their own homes.

Do not wait for anything to happen or to be achieved. The secret of happiness is to be happy today with the little things of today. Look for those little bits of happiness around you in your day-to-day life. If you consciously look at all that is around you, you can discover so many things. The rising sun, a flying bird, a child going to school, an aeroplane, and all such sights can bring joy. Try to revel in these small things of joy.

But why do we ignore or overlook such small bits of happiness? It is partly because we are not conscious of the fact that little everyday things can fill our life with happiness – if only we look around for them. We are too absorbed with ourselves and with mundane things around us that we fail to notice happiness.

This is because of our ego. Our vision is clouded with a bloated image of ourselves. We expect big things to happen to us to bring us happiness. Our ego does not let us take joy in the simple, small things of life. Remember:

Ego is the biggest enemy of happiness.

In the eleventh chapter of the *Bhagavad Gita*, Krishna gives Arjuna a glimpse of His *Viraat-Roop*, a manifestation of His Divine Form. Arjuna finds all human beings including his relatives, friends and enemies gradually drifting towards death (being swallowed by God). Krishna tells Arjuna that even if he does not fight in this battle, all these men would die nevertheless (XII, 32). In fact, they are already dead and Arjuna is merely the instrument, the material cause, and the apparent medium of the action for their death. Therefore, Arjuna should not have this feeling that he is the person who is causing death to anyone. Arjuna should have neither the guilt nor the ego that he is the cause of such action.

Ego emanates out of the sense of insecurity and is the counter-defence mechanism of our survival instinct, born out of fear and weakness. It is a product of self-attachment and a typical characteristic of people with poor self-esteem and an inferiority complex. One who is emotionally weak needs reassurance about his security. Thus, ego makes man possessive and sensitive to attack. It leads to development of feelings of owning, and aggravates the sense of 'I', 'Me' and 'My'. The more we possess, the more secure we feel.

Hence, ego feeds on continuous self-gratification and self-glorification. The egoist wants subservience and flattery from others. Since he does not command respect, he demands respect, even by force. However, while self-gratification satisfies the ego, it has no rejuvenating power. In fact, while such self-exhilaration excites us in the short term, it also carries a subconscious undercurrent of guilt. Thus, the egoistic person is really never a happy person.

According to the philosophy of the *Gita* (II, 71) since attachment is illogical, the ego is also illogical. That is why the yogi treats pleasure and pain, victory and defeat with equal nonchalance. He ruthlessly follows the path of righteousness, which his conscience guides him towards. He acts as his duty demands and is not swayed either by the desires of his senses of pleasure nor does he covet things for selfish gains. Thus, he is free of his nature, of the actions caused by his nature, and of their result as well as of the affectations of the results of his actions. He acts as if he is his own master. He has truly achieved liberation. He is without ego and truly at peace with himself.

In *Ashtavakra Gita,* the king asked the rishi to tell him in a nutshell the way to salvation. The rishi answered: "Give up ego."

Ego binds us to a complicated mix of material and emotional things. In the process, it distorts our vision, develops prejudices, affects our behaviour and rationality, and finally destroys our peace of mind. It is not desirable that the ego should control the mind, because the egoistic person cannot take rational decisions. Nor should ego control our emotions. This leads to inner conflicts and loss of peace of mind. Therefore, try to get rid of ego.

- ❑ **Be humble.** Nothing brings peace of mind as surely as humility does. Humility relieves you from doing lots of things that you do for putting up a pretence of being what you are not, but what you would like others to think you are. You put on a mask and act like a stranger. You behave in a way that is alien to your basic nature. All this play-acting takes a toll on your nerves and your nature. Over a period of time, it distorts your nature and you turn into something you were not, something unnatural. This causes tension and deprives you of peace of mind. In the end, this entire facade does not work, because people come to understand what you really are. They are not fooled. Only, you end up fooling yourself. So be natural, be humble. It is easier to be yourself than to be someone else.
- ❑ **Be simple.** Being simple means depending less and less on extraneous things for happiness. The more simple a life you lead, the less would you depend on external things and the less would be the occasions to make you unhappy. Simplicity should not only be physical in nature, but rather more so, it should be in thoughts also. Get rid of emotional complications and keep your thoughts simple. Do not clutter your mind and emotions with complexes, schemes, grudges, envy, regret, hate and other feelings that only bring unhappiness to you. So, be sincere, straight and simple. It takes less effort and causes less worry.

- **Be polite.** When *Yaksha* asked Yudhishthira (Mahabharata) what was most difficult thing to control, Yudhishthira replied that tongue was most difficult to control. Verily, we often speak out such words, often unnecessarily, that offend others. Impolite language benefits no one, and often in the end causes us grief. We must inculcate a habit of always being polite, even if we are not in a position to do anything else.
- **Be forgiving.** A truly humble man has no cause for grudge or grievance against anyone. When you forgive someone who has caused you hurt, you in fact remove yourself away from the very cause of that hurt. At the time of his crucifixion, Christ forgave his detractors. When you absolve your opponents, you also absolve yourself. But if you carry grudges and the hurt and retain a sense of revenge, you remain in stress, because attaining revenge is also a goalpost, and such a goalpost keeps you unhappy before you pass it, as well as after you have passed it. But forgiving frees you of such negative feelings. So why carry the burden of revenge? Forgive and forget.
- **Be empathetic.** Think of others. Try to see the world standing in the other person's shoes. Try to think what the other person thinks or feels. Life is not just as we see it. There are others also, with almost as much right to live and to view things with their own eyes and from their own perspective. Respect their right to think that way. Only by seeing things from another person's eyes would you be able to see a thing in the correct perspective. Eventually, it would help only you. So why deprive yourself of seeing things in totality?
- **Be considerate.** Happiness is not an island in which you can live alone. Unless you share happiness, it vanishes. The *Gita* states that those who only want to take, without giving back, act like thieves. Thieves are not known to be happy people. So be considerate towards others. Do not be preoccupied all the time

with your own self. You are not that important. You are just one among the billions. Selfishness in any case does not pay in the long run. So try to spread happiness, and you will automatically get much more in return. It is a better investment in time.

- ❑ **Be caring.** You cannot live in society and not care for others. You have to contribute to society as much as you take from society. Have compassion for others. Try to help others in their moments of distress. Caring for others enriches your self-esteem and contributes to your happiness.
- ❑ **Be honest.** Honesty is not just about money. It is about thoughts and character. Honesty is being truthful to your own self. When you try to deceive others, you finally end up deceiving yourself. Honesty is the best policy in more ways than one.
- ❑ **Be generous.** Generosity again is not just about money. Generosity is about magnanimity, about having a large heart, which has ample room for everyone. Generosity is about accepting mistakes and imperfections, whether they are of your own making or of others' making, without being agitated.
- ❑ **Be a learner.** Did you know of Big Bang earlier? Have you heard about Ice Ages? What do you know about tsunami? Expand your horizon. There are so many interesting things to know. Life keeps teaching you new things all the time. At no stage should you feel that you have learnt all that you needed to. Be ready to learn new things at all times. The world of knowledge is continuously expanding. You have to keep pace with the times. Keep educating yourself. Only a dead body does not need any further education. Education widens your thinking and keeps you mentally young and alert. Develop the habit of reading and take an interest in knowing new things.
- ❑ **Be ready to admit mistakes.** Many of us treat life like a battle that has to be won. Actually, there are no victors

in this battle. There are only happy and unhappy people. Therefore, we should not be very stubborn about our ideas. We are all liable to make mistakes. There is no harm in admitting mistakes. The truly stupid person is one who does not realise his mistakes, and not the one who makes mistakes. And if you accept your faults, you not only give yourself an opportunity to improve, but also relieve yourself of the burden of carrying on with the mistakes.

Besides, you really do not lose anything in admitting faults. Overall, you are the biggest gainer, not someone else. So have the courage to admit mistakes that you may make.

- **Be prepared for changes.** The universe is in a constant state of dynamic flux. Everything keeps changing all the time. There is nothing static in this world. New things will come and some of the old things will go, whether these are men or material things. Be prepared for such changes.
- **Live in the present.** The past is dead and gone. Do not carry the burden of the past. Consign the dead to the flames. And as far as the future is concerned, do plan for it, but always live in the present, because the future is always uncertain. The present moment is the most important time for you because that is the only time when you are actually living. The past has already been lived and spent. The future is yet to be lived. So life actually is only the present moment. Make the most of it. Do not let the past or the future overshadow the present. And live each day one at a time.
- **Don't look down upon others.** Do not have a sense of superiority or vanity. Remember that achievements and failures, whether yours or those of someone else, are all due to Nature working on the elements, and that everything is temporary and transitory. You may be intelligent, hard working and may have achieved a lot in life. But does that entitle you to be so proud? After

all, what is your personal contribution for possessing the qualities that you have? You may have been born a mental cripple, without any fault of yours! So where is the room for pride? It is illogical, a very narrow view of the working of the cosmic system, the *Maya*. Things are neither superior nor inferior in this world. Things are only different. And that is Nature.

- ❑ **Don't gloat over others' failures.** Unhappiness in your neighbourhood can certainly waft into your home too. Instead of rejoicing in the defeats of other people, if you try to help them, your self-esteem would rise, and so would your happiness.

> *Be good to others to feel good about yourself.*
> *Whatever increases your self-esteem*
> *increases your happiness.*

- ❑ **Do not** indulge in petty thoughts.
- ❑ **Do not** get irritated over minor things.
- ❑ **Do not** complicate thoughts.

Many of us get into extremely petty mental wranglings over the most insignificant issues. We spoil our own mood and that of others for trivial things. Many of these issues are too insignificant in the total scheme of things. Relieve yourself of such things. You would feel lighter.

After all, what is life? It is a span of time that we have to spend on this earth. And that time is not only limited but is also being continuously spent. With each passing second we have lesser and lesser time left to live.

Should we spend it in worthless mental strife, in poisoning our own thoughts, in activities and pursuits that are likely to make us unhappy?

No!

Life is too short, and too precious, to be wasted on such trivial things. We can consciously rise above such inconsequential matters and assign ourselves a greater role in life. We achieve greatness by thinking high.

Rise above your petty self
and realise your true greatness.

- **Do not expect too much.** By expecting too much from others, we only make ourselves miserable. If you act with any type of expectations, you would be in for disappointment. Do what you have to do as a duty that is to be done, and be done with it. Do not keep expectations lingering in your mind.
- **Laugh.** Do not be so serious. There is nothing to be so serious about. Laugh at yourself more than at others. Realise what sort of complicated and unhappy life you had been living before you read this book. And now that you have understood this, laugh at your own behaviour, at your own actions. Laughing at your own self will relieve you of all your troubles and completely de-stress you. Tell others why you are laughing and try to spread sunshine everywhere.

Do not fear anything.
Seek the joy of life.
Keep things simple.
Generate love, compassion, harmony
and forgiveness in your life.
Seek the brighter side.

When you see dark clouds,
look for the rainbow...

And you will always be happy.

■■

कुछ उत्कृष्ट पुस्तकें

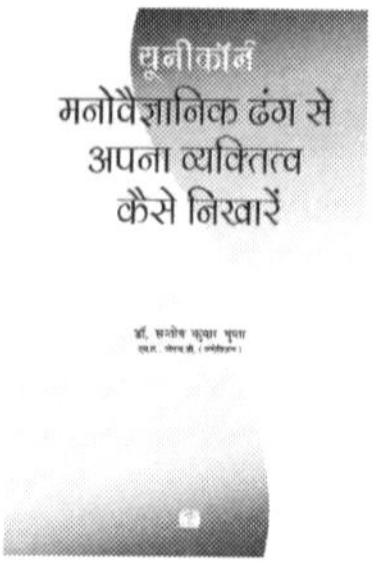

9378 A • ₹ 96/-

मनोवैज्ञानिक ढंग से अपना व्यक्तित्व कैसे निखारें

समाज में प्रत्येक व्यक्ति का अपना व्यक्तित्व होता है, जो एक-दूसरे से अलग होता है। प्रत्येक व्यक्ति अपने व्यक्तित्व से दूसरे व्यक्ति को प्रभावित करने की चेष्टा करता है। कुछ का व्यक्तित्व स्वत: इतना प्रभावी होता है कि वह दूसरे के व्यक्तित्व पर छा जाता है और कुछ का व्यक्तित्व आत्महीनता से ग्रसित होने के कारण दूसरे के समक्ष दब जाता है। ऐसे में वह पूर्ण सफल नहीं होता और अपनी आकांक्षाओं को पूर्ण नहीं कर पाता।

व्यक्तित्व क्या है? 'व्यक्तित्व' व्यक्ति की वेशभूषा मात्र नहीं है, अपितु वह व्यक्ति के रूप-रंग, चाल-ढाल, व्यवहार और आन्तरिक गुणों की सम्मिलित इकाई है, जो प्रथम दृष्टि में ही दिख जाती है, महसूस की जाती है। जो दिखते ही प्रभावित कर दे, उसका व्यक्तित्व अच्छा माना जाता है।

इस पुस्तक में लेखक ने मनोवैज्ञानिक तरीके से व्यक्तित्व को निखारने व प्रभावशाली बनाने के तरीके बताए हैं, जिन्हें अपनाकर आप भी अपने व्यक्तित्व में निखार लाकर उसे प्रभावशाली बना सकते हैं। अत: व्यक्तित्व में निखार लाने के लिए इस पुस्तक को अवश्य पढ़ें।

सफलता एक प्रक्रिया है, घटना नहीं!

9382 A • ₹ 96/-

विश्व की हर वस्तु एक प्रक्रिया से होकर गुजरती है, चाहे वह वस्तु प्राकृतिक हो या भौतिक। यहाँ तक कि काल्पनिक रचनाओं की भी एक निश्चित प्रक्रिया है। जो लोग इसे समझ लेते हैं, उनके लिए सफलता प्राप्त करना सरल हो जाता है और जो नहीं समझते, उनके लिए जटिल। प्रत्येक व्यक्ति सफल होना चाहता है, परन्तु क्या वह सफलता के लिए तैयार है?

घटनाएं स्वयं नहीं घटतीं, उन्हें आपको घटाना पड़ता है। सफलता के शिखर तक पहुंचने के लिए आपको एक-एक सीढ़ी चढ़ना होगा। यदि छलागें मारते हुए कई-कई सीढ़ियाँ चढ़ें, तो न केवल जमीन पर दोबारा आ गिरने की संभावना है, अपितु चोट लगने की भी प्रबल संभावना है। अतः सफलता की सीढ़ियाँ चढ़ना शुरू करने से पहले, यह जानना जरूरी है कि कितनी सीढ़ियाँ हैं और आप कहाँ पहुंचेंगे?

विश्व में 20 प्रतिशत लोग ही वास्तविक सफलता प्राप्त कर पाते हैं। क्या वे इसके लिए किसी विशेष प्रक्रिया से गुजरते हैं? क्या एक आम आदमी इस प्रक्रिया को अपनाकर उतनी ही बड़ी सफलता प्राप्त कर सकता है? क्या यह वास्तव में संभव है? इन्हीं सब प्रश्नों का उत्तर देने का प्रयास है, यह पुस्तक... 'सफलता एक प्रक्रिया है, घटना नहीं!' जीवन में सफल होने के लिए इस पुस्तक को अवश्य पढ़ें।

New Arrivals

9394 A • ₹ 150/-

Life An Odyssey

Time-tested Mantras Providing Solutions to Life's Problems

Life is a mystery for those who keep running behind their expectations, ignoring the need to explore their soul and the happiness therein. Exploring the soul needs reflection. Reflection leads to realization, realization leads to wisdom and wisdom is the path to enlightenment.

Life-An Odyssey is a choice selection of 35 musings. Each musing provides an introspective path to successfully overcome the different challenges that everyone encounters.

The Tao of CONFIDENCE

Featuring wonderful exercises to achieve mega success

The most comprehensive and powerful manual ever written on the subject of self-confidence. Self-confidence is not an inborn trait or a quality but a practical set of thoughts, beliefs, habits and behaviours which can be learned, in an organised step-by-step format by anyone desiring to create the life of one's deepest dreams.

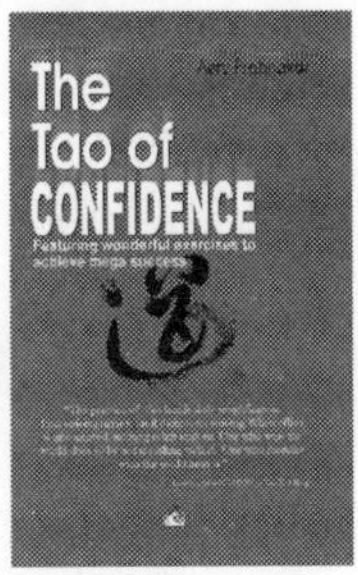

9389 D • ₹ 96/-

9336 B • ₹ 135/-

100 Minutes

That'll Change The Way You Live!

Real life, at times, tends to get mundane and boring.

How to survive against such inertia and overwhelming odds in life is the mool mantra of this unique little book.

These 'top tips' will help you live life more peacefully and more successfully, whether you are young or old, man or woman, businessman or executive, professional or in service.

This is real stuff for real people no lectures, no empty talk, only immensely practical wisdom! That too told in a humorous way by the author who has himself learnt them in the process of surviving some great crises in life, and thus speaks with the authority of personal experience.